WHITE STAR
PUBLIERS

CONTENTS

INTRODUCTION   PAGE 8

SUGAR CANE AND FREEDOM   PAGE 22

THE SURREAL METROPOLIS   PAGE 46

CHARACTERISTIC CITIES AND VILLAGES   PAGE 70

A NATURAL ENVIRONMENT WORTH SAVING   PAGE 100

THE CUBANIA: A UNIQUE CULTURE   PAGE 126

Graphic design
Patrizia Balocco

© 2004 White Star S.r.l.
Via Candido Sassone, 22/24
13100 Vercelli, Italy
www.whitestar.it

TRANSLATION:
AMY CHRISTINE EZRIN

ISBN 88-544-0040-8

REPRINTS:
1 2 3 4 5 6   08 07 06 05 04

Printed in China
Color separation: Grafotitoli, Milan

Cuba

PLACES AND HISTORY

Text by Paolo Giunta La Spada

1 Ernesto "Che" Guevara – one of the 20th century's photographic icons – commemorated by an unknown mural painter, in a street in Camagüey, central Cuba.

2-7 In this 18th-century print, the English, in 1762, form ranks in front of Havana, snatched from the Spanish and occupied for a year. By that time, Spanish power was in decline.

3-6 Within the barrier reef, the ocean waves gradually diminish until they lap the beach of Cayo Coco, on Cuba's northern coast. This cayo is one of the island's biggest.

INTRODUCTION

8 top left Big tourist resorts are becoming ever more numerous on Cuba. Seen here, a resort in Cayo Coco, in the province of Ciego de Ávila.

8 top right Beyond the inhabited areas, Cayo Coco has remained unspoiled. The cayos are essential sites for marine bird reproduction.

*I*t was October 27, 1492. For Christopher Columbus, it had been a good day at sea. In the afternoon, he had sighted a long and solid stretch of coastline. It has been about two weeks since that legendary October 12, when the Genoese navigator "discovered" the new land, called it San Salvador, and sailed out to the open sea, happy to have avoided a mutiny among his crew and to have restocked his ship with food and water.

He was convinced that he had discovered the western route to the Indies, but he was not satisfied with having landed on only a small island; he wanted to reach the continental coast of Asia. On the evening of October 27, 1492, as the sunset tinted the sky orange, he disembarked on the shore of present-day Bariay, on the northeast side of the island of Cuba. Columbus christened the island "Juana," in honor of the first-born heir to the Spanish throne, son of King Ferdinand

8 bottom The famous Playa de los Flamencos, or Flamenco Beach, is one of the more secluded ones in the Cayo Coco area.

and Queen Isabella, henceforth considering it a new colonial possession. He explored its northern perimeter and, satisfactorily noting the vastness of the territory, proudly declared it to be the eastern shore of Asia. More than five centuries have passed since October 27, 1492, but the magic and unique character of Cuba continue to enchant. Its 4,194 islands, including the smallest and tiniest *cayos* and *cayuelos*, constitute an archipelago of natural settings unique in all the world.

9 A hotel dominates the palm-tree groves on the coast of Varadero, the pride of the new Cuban economy based on the tourism industry. A good number of the island's hotels are concentrated in this area, which, however, is forbidden to Cubans.

The people who populate Cuba are of American, African, and European descent, they also include a minority group of Asian origin. Cuba is, therefore, the result of an encounter, concentrated over time, between peoples of different cultures who have been forced to co-ex-

ist owing to dramatic historical events that began with the island's colonial conquest and the slavery that followed. Cuba is a bridge between diverse identities, a social, cultural, and artistic laboratory, in perennial turmoil and continuous transformation. Throughout the island, all year round, cultural initiatives, music festivals, art exhibits, film festivals, conferences, and meetings proceed at a feverish pace.

Yet, in no city in this land does time appear as still and crystallized as on the

"marvelous island." The colonial towns are intact and perfectly preserved. Hardly tampered with, the architecture reflects the various epochs in which the stately buildings were constructed, with their marble courtyards flooded with light open to the sea breeze and their majestic gardens designed by great masters. Huge automobiles from the 1950s blend into the landscape as if they were monuments to a surreal kind of urban charm. The working-class neighborhoods look similar to those of Mediter-

ranean cities where time also seems to stand still and suspended: in the aroma of freshly-roasted coffee, just-baked bread, roasting meat on Sundays and holidays, and fresh fruit sold at the market, complete with the raised voices of the vendors and the sounds of the ever-present music.

Another critical element in understanding Cuba is the sensation of eternal summer: the humidity that scents towels and weaves its way into clothes, the naked backs of men working or sitting in

11 top Colonial-era buildings surround Plaza Mayor, in Santa Clara. In this city, now the location of many industries and a university, Che Guevara had his final victory over the forces of the dictator Fulgencio Batista.

11 center The sun casts a golden hue over the mixture of modern and colonial buildings on the Malecón, Havana's famous seafront drive.

11 bottom At the sound of the drums, a group of musicians in costume take part in the desfile, *the parade of floats at Carnival, in the streets of Havana. Unlike other Catholic countries, in Cuba this holiday falls in the middle of summer.*

front of their house, the perennially light and flimsy cottons worn by girls, the constant search for shade, the afternoon nap taken to avoid the hottest hours of the day, the evening walks along the shore with friends or in couples, and the fans of the ladies at the theater. A country's philosophy of life can show itself in a restaurant where an early-1900s atmosphere is still found, with slow service like in a city café in Africa, aristocratic waiters like in old Europe, and the happiness of a time long gone.

10 left Calixto Carcia, another hero of the Cuban independence, is portrayed in the garden named after him in Holguín, in the western part of the island.

10-11 White marble and a statuesque tension characterize the base of this Havana monument to General Máximo Gómez, the hero of the two wars of independence.

The social dimension is exhibited in the pride of a people who have fought for over 150 years for their freedom and independence, and that will not give up the desire to build values and give meaning to their lives, even if it means isolation and sacrifice. Cuba's main economic partner was Communist Russia, with which it conducted 85 percent of its commerce. With the collapse of the Soviet Union in 1989, it seemed that the Cuban economic and political system was bound to cave in. In those years, the United States, rather than open up politically to Havana, reinforced its embargo, a total economic boycott of its small neighbor, despite the opposition of the United Nations. Cuba overcame the crisis by opening its doors to tourists, promoting private agricultural produce, and decriminalizing the possession of dollars by Cuban citizens. Today, the economy has begun to grow again thanks to foreign investment in tourism and construction, even though the lines of people holding their *libreta*, the Cuban monthly rations card, indicate a country still far from prosperous. President Fidel Castro has led Cuba since 1959, convinced that history is on his side.

Havana

Matanzas

Varadero

Cárdenas

Sabana Archipelago

Viñales

Sierra del Rosario

Pinar del Río

Sierra de los Organos

Peninsula de Zapata

Santa Clara

Placeta

Cienfuegos

Bahía de Cachinos (Bay of Pigs)

Sierra del Escambray

San Juan

Trinidad

Santa Barbara

Nueva Gerona

Santa Fé

Isla de la Juventud

CARIBBEAN SEA

Certainly, with the increase in tourism on the island, interest in understanding the reality of the Cuban people's lives has grown. Visitors feel like they are in a "film" from the past: nestled in a sidecar, a white-haired woman passes down a street, a girl looks at the tourist with naked femininity, a young man shows off how macho he is with his sculpted muscles, a band of old men play a classic mambo in a bar where Ernest Hemingway's favorite cocktail is still drunk, and in the souvenir shops, the portrait of Che Guevara still stands out on calendars, posters, and t-shirts. To experience Cuba close-up and try to grasp its spirit, it is necessary to abandon the common "pro" and "con" logic of political concepts and rise above the stereotypical view centered on clubs, pretty girls, and white beaches. Otherwise, justice is not done to the poignant beauty of such a unique country and to its unusual, diverse, and complex nature, with a history full of contradictions and without guarantees.

Cuba has the timeless appeal of unique and singular objects, the appeal held by gems that will never be sold, the charm of that which can only be loved and lived, though André Breton, the famous French artist, once said that Cuba is too surreal a place to live there. Cuba is in the love songs of César Portillo, in the colorful canvases of René Portocarrero, in the pace of a factory worker's hard labor, in the little girls who go to school wearing red handkerchiefs around their necks, in the counters of the Art Deco bars serving the world's best rum, in the monthly eight-egg allowance obtained with the *libreta* for 80 peso cents, in the aroma of a neighbor's cigar that lets one know whether he is home or not, in the rich narratives of Alejo Carpentier, in the salty air that devours the houses, and in the spiritual state that pervades all who live there. Christopher Columbus saw the matter correctly when, a few days after that Saturday, October 27, 1492, with his eyes filled by a kaleidoscope of unique colors, he wrote in his damp and yellowed captain's log that he had visited "the most beautiful land that human eyes had ever seen." There could be no better introduction to a book on Cuba than this comment written by the great Italian navigator.

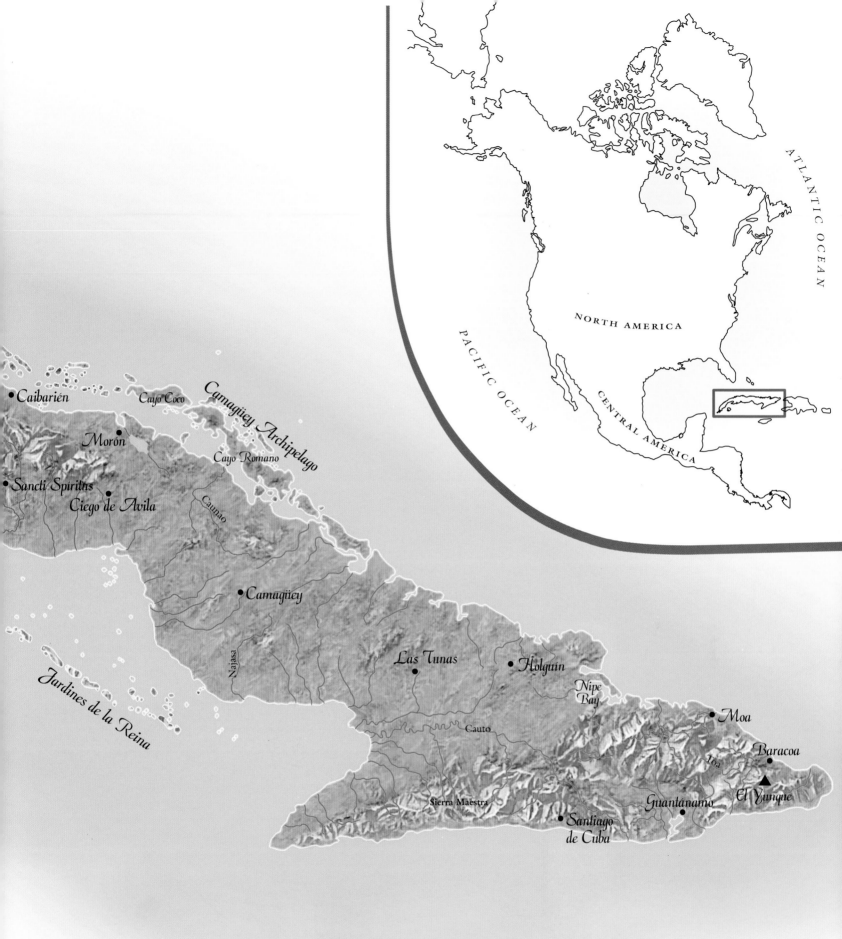

Caibarién

Cayo Coco

Camagüey Archipelago

Morón

Cayo Romano

Sancti Spíritus

Ciego de Ávila

Caunao

Camagüey

Najasa

Jardines de la Reina

Las Tunas

Holguín

Nipe Bay

Moa

Cauto

Toa

Baracoa

Sierra Maestra

Guantánamo

El Yunque

Santiago de Cuba

NORTH AMERICA

ATLANTIC OCEAN

PACIFIC OCEAN

CENTRAL AMERICA

16-17 The planted farms on this valley floor are overlooked by the spurs of the Sierra del Escambray, which peaks west of Cienfuegos at 3,763 feet.

18-19 The Capitol steals the show from the eclectic edifices found in Havana's government district. They were mostly built in the 1920s and 30s.

20-21 A traveling musician with his instrument on a beach and an enormous 1950s-era car unwittingly and inadvertently represent symbols of the reality, or the myth, of Cuba.

SUGAR CANE AND FREEDOM

Studies supported by the carbon-dating of fossilized human settlements confirm that the island of Cuba has been populated since 2000 B.C. It is believed, however, to have been inhabited since 3500-3000 B.C., but to date no proof has been found. Gatherers, and then fishermen and hunters, permanently occupied Cuba, attracted by its landscape featuring thousands of islands immersed in coral-lined lagoons, fertile land and green hills, lush forests, and coastal inlets sheltered from the wind. The Guanahatabey settled to the west, the Siboney in the center and to the east. Over

successive migrations, they were joined by the Arawak, a Taíno-speaking people that constituted the most widespread ethnic group in the Caribbean during the pre-Columbian era. Besides being hunters and fishermen, the Arawak were small-scale farmers. They grew grain, sweet and plain potatoes, cassava, squash, nuts, and pepper. In their villages, built of wood and straw, avocado trees and tobacco plants always grew. They did not know how to write, work with metal, or raise livestock, but they worked stone with great skill, fired clay pots, and fished using a fish with suckers. Over time, the Arawak came under great pressure from Carib peoples arriving from the archipelagos of northern South America and were forced to move *en masse* in migratory waves to Cuba, where the open spaces protected by impenetrable forests offered them good odds for defending themselves against outside attacks. When Columbus landed on Cuba, the island's autochthonous population numbered about 100,000 people, 75 percent of whom were Taíno-speaking Arawaks. Fortunately for them, the Spanish's earliest gold-seeking expeditions produced negative results, and the *conquistadors* moved their business interests to Santo Domingo. In 1508, Sebastian de Ocampo circumnavigated the territory, thus proving that Cuba was an island. Four years later, in 1512, Diego Velásquez de Cuéllar endeavored to conquer the island with 300 soldiers, including a few of the *conquistadors* who would become notorious throughout South America such as Pánfilo de Narváez, Juan de Grijalba, Pedro de Alvarado, and Hernán Cortés.

24 *The Caribbean and Cuba, Central America with Mexico and Guatemala, and South America with Peru are illustrated in the 1563* Atlas of the Universe *by Lazare Luis. Only the colonized regions appear clearly outlined, whereas the southern areas of the American continent remain undefined, even though Magellan had found the passage between the Atlantic and Pacific oceans in 1520.*

25 top *In 1542, the monk Bartolomé de La Casas sent King Charles V his A* Short Account of the Destruction of the Indies, *his defense against accusations made by Spanish colonizers about his conversion methods. Between 1553 and 1561, he recounted the conquest from 1492 to 1520 in the* History of the Indies, *developing the idea of the "gentle and good by nature" Indian.*

25 bottom *After the conquest of Mexico and Peru, the Spanish government decided that all ships about to return to Old Spain loaded with treasure would have to stop at the port of Havana. Thus, the city's wealth grew quickly, such that it also, unfortunately, became prey to ferocious pirate attacks, as shown in this illustration.*

By the end of 1514, Velásquez and his men had settled themselves on a large part of the island and had begun to build its first cities: Nuestra Asunción de Baracoa, Santiago de Cuba, Bayamo, Santa María de Puerto Principe, Sancti Spiritus, Santisima Trinidad, and San Cristóbal de la Habana. The names of the earliest towns corroborate the ideological rationalization behind the massacres committed by the Spanish of the *Indios*, so-called by Columbus in his belief that they were "inhabitants of the Indies." As in later historical eras, conversion to Christianity provided an excuse to kill, destroy, and burn. It involved "bringing civilization" to "peoples without God." The opinion of those peoples counted little in the face of a set of absolute values that could not be questioned. Thousands of natives were massacred despite the rebellion of some of the *caciques*, or tribal chiefs, such as Hatuey, the bold leader who mounted resistance to the invaders but was forced to surrender, and later burned at the stake. The monk Bartolomé de las Casas wrote that a Catholic priest asked Hatuey, as he was being tortured, if he wanted to convert in order to go to heaven. With the flames already flickering at his feet, Hatuey asked if the Spanish could also go to heaven. When the priest answered yes, the chief Hatuey stated that he never wanted to meet them again and resolutely refused conversion. Bartolomé de las Casas denounced the violent acts perpetrated by the *conquistadors* and called for the abolition of the *encomienda* system, under

which the Indians were forced to work without pay for the Spanish, with the excuse that they were receiving Christian teachings. The *encomienda* system was abolished in 1542, but systematic exploitation of the Indians continued. Another scourge brought by the Spanish, smallpox, combined with the massacres to reduce the Indian population to about 5,000 individuals by the mid-sixteenth century. From 1522 on, Africans were shipped to Cuba to be used as slaves to work the fields, to excavate mineral deposits, and to build the cities. It is important to note that the earliest slave shipments to Cuba were distinguished by the fact that entire tribes were moved without being separated upon arrival. This allowed for the preservation of cultures that would otherwise have become extinct. In other regions

of the Americas, and later on also in Cuba, the traders of humans adopted the horrible practice of forming groups of slaves composed of individuals who spoke different languages. This was done in order to prevent any form of communication among the slaves and to reduce the risk of rebellion. Competition between Spain, England, France, Holland, and Portugal promoted the spread of piracy. Smuggling stolen goods was a flourishing business practiced even by the Spanish in Cuba to the detriment of the mother country, which was accused of imposing a strict monopoly and heavy taxes. Many cites were pillaged and burned by wretchedly famous pirates such as Gilberto Girón, Jean David Nau (alias François L'Olonnais), Henry Morgan, and Francis Drake. There were also Spanish pirates and one Cuban, Diego Grillo. All ships without a military escort were attacked, and every European fleet kept track of pirates and buccaneers present in the region. In 1604, a black slave killed Gilberto Girón during an attack and freed the bishop, Juan de las Cabezas Altamirano, who had been kidnapped by the pirates. In honor of this act of courage, the poet Silvestre de Balboa, originally from the Canary Islands and an inhabitant of Puerto Principe, composed the first poetic verse ever written in Cuba, a fragment of which reads,

An Ethiopian worthy of praise

By the name of Salvador, a bold and brave Negro

Of those who own Yara in his land,

Son of Galomón, an elder wise man....

26 top Illegal trade and smuggling were widespread, as this 17th-century print shows: European merchants negotiate with the Indians for bundles and bushels of sugar. Often the anchoring spots of pirates were secretly patrolled by the same authorities as in the port, who were well aware of the contents of the ships' holds.

26-27 The siege of Havana, illustrated in this 1767 English oil painting on canvas, was marked by the Spanish decision to bar the port crosswise with two large ships rather than let the British fleet enter and be met by a host of fortified lines. The decision was also influenced by their wish to protect the precious cargo of about 100 ships at dock.

27 left The production of sugar contributed to Cuba's great commercial success. To harvest the cane and grind its fibers, slave and animal labor was exploited, as seen in this print of French origin dated 1759, which reproduces and illustrates a period mill.

27 right The historian Irene Wright claims that the castles erected to protect Havana (the plan of a fort is shown) are monuments to Francis Drake, who stopped his attacks on the city in 1586 upon seeing its new fortifications. The very same forts were, however, useless during the English assault of 1762 because the city was invaded by land.

MOULIN A SUCRE.

A. *Chassis avec les Tambours* G. *Les Coyaux*
B. *Poteaux* H. *L'Enrayeure*
C. *Sablière* L. *Le Poinçon*
D. *Les Forces* M. *La Damoiselle*
E. *L'Entrait* N. *Bras de Moulin*
F. *Les Chevrons* O. *Chevaux qui tirent le Moulin*

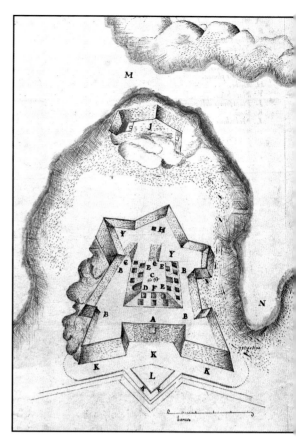

To combat constant pirate attacks, the Spanish government began to undertake the fortification of the most important ports. Thus, the fortresses La Fuerza, La Punta, El Morro in Havana, and El Morro in Santiago came to be. In 1762, on the eve of war between Spain and England, Havana had a population between 30,000 and 40,000 people, more than Boston or New York, and was the third-largest city in terms of population in the New World, exceeded only by Lima and Mexico City. To oppose the alliance between the France and Spain, the British declared war against Spain on January 4, 1762. Britain was emerging as the greatest colonial power in the world; they had defeated the French and had conquered India and Canada. The British government did not want to leave the most important port in the Americas in Spanish hands. On March 5, 1762, an impressive and well-equipped fleet secretly set sail from Portsmouth. In Jamaica, it boarded additional military forces, slaves, ammunition, and considerable quantities of rum, and then steered for Cuba. The Spanish command was warned only one day before the arrival of the English, and the siege of Havana, begun in June, ended in the conquest of the city on August 13, 1762, following bitter fighting. The British did not occupy all of the island, but only the tract of coastline that ran from the port of Mariel, 34 miles west of Havana, to the city of Matanzas, 65 miles to the east. The Spanish moved the capital to Santiago and continued to govern most of the Cuban territory, whereas in Havana, now under British control, commerce came back to life, newly free of the threat of piracy, which the British had sustained and protected for so long. In 1763, with the Treaty of Versailles that declared peace between France, Spain, and Britain, the British took Florida from the Spanish and Havana returned to Spain after eleven months of British occupation. The freedom of trade inherited from the British was partially maintained by the Spain of Charles III, and after the United States obtained independence from Great Britain in 1783, Cuba managed to overtake Jamaica in supplying sugar to the United States. The cultivation of sugar cane continued at high levels, while the importation and exploitation of slaves increased. In 1791, when an unstoppable slave revolt broke out in nearby Haiti, the big French plantation-owners who had initiated the cultivation of coffee and expanded sugar-cane production from 11,000 tons in 1778 to 36,000 tons in 1799 and 45,000 tons in 1802 took refuge on Cuba.

28 top *In July of 1839, a revolt broke out on the slave ship* Amistad. *The 53 slaves on board threw the captain into the sea and forced its owners, to set sail for Africa. After two months, the ship landed near New York. The 35 surviving slaves were tried and acquitted, and thanks to the help of a rich anti-slavery activist, returned to Sierra Leone.*

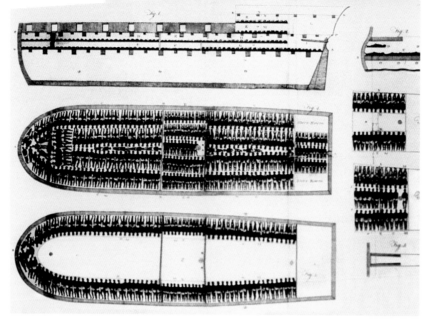

workers independence movements in South America and the wide-ranging echo of revolutionary industrial and political changes in Europe and the United States. Even the Masonic lodges in Cuba conspired against Madrid. Though numerous attempts to rebel failed, leaders emerged from the period, such as the priest Felix Varela and the poet José María Heredia, who were able to spark a new national political consciousness in the Cuban people. Varela, a teacher at the San Carlos Seminary in Havana, supported Reformist ideas and was convinced that independence was necessary for progress in

28-29 This reproduction of a 1950 poster illustrates a scene dating back to 1840: naked children, girls, and men are seen sold as slaves in Havana, at the corner of Calle Officio and San Francisco Square, not far from the port.

29 top This illustration reproduces the lengthwise section and cross section of a ship used to transport slaves. Merchants crammed human beings onto their vessels like any other goods. This traffic involved the western coast of Africa from Senegal in the north as far as Angola, in the south.

29 bottom In the second half of the 19th century, slave traders often worked clandestinely, combining more and more frequently their infamous trade with acts of piracy. This engraving shows the capture of a ship carrying slaves.

Between 1770 and 1800, more slaves were brought to the island than in the three previous centuries combined. Three trends interested the Creole middle class in the early years of the 19th century. The first was the idea of being annexed by the United States, which was echoed by the politics of the American presidents and supported by the large-scale producers who had the most intense economic relationships with North America. The second trend was that of the independence movement, which, however, counted few followers, considering that the big landowners and the upper class largely held ultraconservative positions that looked unfavorably on big changes. The third, predominant among the rich Creoles at the time, was the Reformism trend, which claimed that the times were ripe for liberal political reforms of moderate scope. Starting in 1820, the first uprisings to achieve freedom from Spanish domination broke out in Cuba; they were primarily influenced by

his country. Once he became a member of the parliament in 1822, he proposed the abolition of slavery and defended the people's right to self-determination, in keeping with resolutions already passed by many European nations.

He was condemned to death and forced to escape to the United States. Heredia took part in the fight for independence when 18 years old as a militant member of the secret society Soles y Rayos de Bolívar and wrote poetic works of high formal quality and intense feeling. These are some lines from his poem *Hymn of the Exile*:

Cuba! At last, you will see yourself free and pure
  like the air of light you breathe,
  like the boiling waves you watch
  kiss the sand of your shores.
  Although vile traitors serve
  the tyrant, rage is useless;
It is not in vain that 'twixt Cuba and Spain the broad sea tends its waves.

While the desire for independence that flowed through the people's blood was being repressed, many sugar-cane plantation owners plotted ways for Cuba to be annexed by the United States. For the large-scale producers the advantages were many; the United States, unlike the European powers, was in favor of preserving slavery and appeared to have the authority needed to guide the fragile Cuban political situation. The American political position, which sought to wipe out the Spanish presence in the Americas, could be summed up by the Monroe Doctrine: America for the Americans. In 1847, armed attempts to bring Cuba under the aegis of the United States began. Groups of mercenaries led by the reactionary General Narciso Lopéz attacked the island several times but without success, and Lopéz, captured by the Spanish, was condemned to death by garrote. The revolt of the slaves, who made up about 58 percent of the Cuban population in 1840 or so, inflamed the rural regions while the political clash between conservatives and reformists increased in intensity. The reformists were themselves divided between those who advocated loyalty to Spain, those who supported annexation to the United States, and fighters for independence. After years of political struggle, on October 10, 1869, on the La Demajagua Farm in the Bayamo area, Carlos Manuel de Céspedes freed his 30 slaves and enlisted them in a group of 147 men, thus starting the war for the liberation of his homeland. In January 1869, the revolutionaries had ready 13,500 cavalry and 20,000 foot soldiers. The war, ferociously brutal, lasted ten years. They turned out to be vague on the issue of abolishing slavery and incapable of leading the offensive in the northern part of the island, where sugar-cane production proceeded undisturbed. Among the rebel leaders, two in particular stood out. They were the Dominican official Máximo Gómez Báez, and Ignazio Agramonte from Camagüey, who espoused Enlightenment ideas and demonstrated great daring on the battle field. On 11 February 1878, the Spanish got their conditions accepted with the Zanjón Pact: the war was over after having cut down 208,000 victims among the Spanish and 50,000 among the Cuban rebels. Antonio Maceo, a mulatto from Santiago, had become a general thanks to his giftedness and great courage. He had also lost his father and 15 of his 18 siblings in the war. After the death of Céspedes and Agramonte in battle, he was the most capable and experienced leader left. At Baraguá, he rejected the imposed peace treaty and reorganized the clandestine network of rebels abroad. Another 15-year-old, José Martí from Havana, had participated in the war for freedom. Born to Spanish parents, taken prisoner and condemned to forced labor, deported to Spain, and then exiled to Mexico and the United States, he was a tireless organizer in the movement for Cuban independence.

30 During the first war of independence, the Cubans burned plantations and sugar mills, like this one near Trinidad, thus liberating the slaves on the destroyed properties and enrolling them in the army fighting for independence. Many landowners did not want to join the movement in order to safeguard their wealth and possessions.

30-31 José Martí, in the middle wearing a black bow tie, poses with his companions at the beginning of the second war of independence. The son of Spanish parents, Martí left behind an abundant legacy of essays, letters, diaries, short stories, children's stories, and poems imbued with a romantic and passionate lyricism.

31 top left This lithograph, produced by the Cuban community of New York in 1896, portrays the heroes of the island's independence: the father of the homeland José Martí, the commander Máximo Gómez, the legendary Antonio Maceo, the president of the first Republic of Cuba Salvador Cisneros, and General Calisto Garcia.

31 top right In the December 27, 1896 edition, the French newspaper Le Petit Parisien *portrayed the dispute between Cuban patriots and the Spanish troops of General Weiler for possession of the remains of Antonio Maceo, the legendary "Bronze Titan" who, over the course of his life, took part in 900 battles for the freedom of his people.*

He succeeded in achieving the abolition of slavery in Cuba in 1886, though the economic influence of the United States, which by 1895 had $50 million invested in Cuba, was constantly becoming more dominant within the island. Without slaves, many old plantation owners sought to change the methods they used to harvest sugar cane and operate the refineries, but they went bankrupt, strangled by debts to rich American investors, who then became the new bosses of the sugar and tobacco industries. On February 24, 1895, Cuba's

second war of independence broke out. On May 19, Spanish troops surprised a detachment of rebels, in the process killing José Martí, the apostle of Cuba's freedom. In October, the forces for independence, led by Máximo Gómez Báez and Antonio Maceo, skillfully invaded Cuba's wealthy western regions. The rebels' military campaign continued to enjoy great success even though on December 7, 1897, at San Pedro, 12 miles southwest of Havana, the legendary commander Antonio Maceo and Panchito, the son of Máximo Gómez Báez, were killed. On February 15, 1898, the American battleship *Maine*, anchored

off the coast of Havana, mysteriously exploded; 266 American sailors died. The Spanish authorities claimed that the explosion originated in the ship's ammunitions hold, but the United States declared war against Spain. The Spanish army was worn out by the attacks of Cuban patriots and the United States' naval blockade. On July 3, 1898, the American fleet opened fire on the old Spanish ships, setting them ablaze. The Cuban victory, accomplished in the field at the high price of so much spilled blood, turned into a victory for the United States as well. On December 10, 1898, the American government forced Spain to accept the Peace of Paris, prohibiting the Cubans from attending the negotiations. On December 28, 1898, Máximo Gómez Báez, the Cuban commander, declared that the island was "neither free nor independent" and that the fight for independence would continue. The Platt Amendment of February 25, 1901 relating to the American military budget stated "the government of Cuba consents that the United States may exercise the right to intervene for the preservation of Cuban independence [and] the maintenance of a government adequate for the protection of life, property, and individual liberty." Cuba was prohibited from entering into international treaties or contracting loans without Washington's approval, and the United States was able to open military bases such as the still occupied one at Guantánamo Bay. In Cuba, the American administration disarmed the population and dissolved all local authorities in order to reorganize control around corrupt pro-United-States governors and police forces that had no other duty than repressing political notions calling for autonomy from the United States. In the early years of the twentieth century, Cuba emerged exhausted from the war: either in battle or by hunger, it had lost 400,000 inhabitants, 75 percent of its livestock, 80 percent of its sugar mills and tobacco-producing facilities, and the sugar-cane crop had been reduced by two thirds. The population of the island numbered just over 1.5 million. For these reasons, in the wake of such ruin, many Cubans actually saw the United States' intervention as positive in that it brought the possibility of development.

Between 1902 and 1905, American industrialists brought 80 percent of mining yields, 25 percent of the sugar plantations, and 90 percent of the tobacco industry under their control. Racial discrimination against black people was vicious. In 1912, the army massacred 3,000 demonstrating Afro-Cubans, and in Pinar del Río, American troops were sent in to put down a revolt of ex-slaves. From 1919 to 1933, during the United States' Prohibition era, North-American tourism based on alcohol consumption, gambling, and prostitution became widespread in Cuba. On May 20, 1925, General Gerardo Machado took power, governing in accordance with the American business community's wishes,

and going so far as to use terror to repress popular rebellion and eliminate union leaders. On September 4, 1933, a coup d'état led by subordinate officers resulted in the general's replacement by Fulgencio Batista who, having disbanded a provisional government that would have improved legal conditions for workers, reinstated the previous pro-American political practices that were subject all kinds of corruption, and took violent repressive reactions against the workers' movement. The Communist Party, born in 1925, enjoyed a strong following, and the international situation, with fascism and nazism in the process of winning power in Italy and Germany, underlined the need for an alliance between antifascist forces throughout the world. Some 800 Cubans went to fight Franco's Nationalists in Spain, and in January 1939, thousands of union delegates met in Havana to create the Workers Confederation of Cuba. Batista decided to open up to some democratic changes, and allowed a new constitution to be written that granted equality for all citizens and established an eight-hour workday. In the 1940s, even some Communist organizations, like the Communist Revolutionary Union Party, supported his populist-style politics. Batista won the 1940 elections and, during the World War II, backed up the Allied forces against the activities of German submarines in the Caribbean. In 1944, new elections took place, but the candidate backed by Batista was defeated. The administrations that followed, those of Ramón Grau San Martín and Carlos Prío Socarrás, were characterized by inefficiency, corruption, and anti-union political crimes. On March 10, 1952, a new coup d'état brought Batista back into power, and two weeks later, the United States officially recognized his government. Batista revoked the 1940 constitution and instituted a government that, despite eliminating civil liberties and political parties, left several Communist advocates, for a certain period, in positions that they had previously held at the Ministry of Labor. The dictator seemed different: he wasted hours on minor issues such as writing a letter or properly tying his tie and spent days playing canasta and watching horror films. He filled the army with his

faithful while the gangsters who backed him drove around Havana in luxurious Cadillacs. Within a few months, the dubious equilibrium was upset by the efforts of rebellious university students who condemned the crimes committed by Batista.

34 top In the presence of the authorities, the United States general and governor of Cuba Leonard Wood and the appointed president Tomas Estrada Palma inaugurated the Republic of Cuba on May 20, 1902.

34 bottom Gerardo Machado y Morales, in good relations with the United States, was openly supported by the American government and Electric Bond and Share, which financed his electoral campaign.

34-35 The people of Havana were enraged by the anti-union policies of Gerardo Machado. The most violent outbreaks occurred in the summer of 1933: on August 12, Machado was forced to abandon Cuba as the American ambassador Benjamin Sumner Welles called for rapid intervention by the United States Navy.

35 bottom Fulgencio Batista participated in the elections of July 15, 1940. Of humble origins, he made his career in the army thanks to his charm and boldness. Referring to 1933, he stated "the revolution was carried out not to eliminate a dictator, but to erase a colonial system that had suffocated the country for 31 years."

In Havana, students, militants from the Orthodox Party, and young Communists formed a small revolutionary group; it was led by Abel Santamaría, his sister Haydée, Melba Hernández, and a young, 27-year-old lawyer by the name of Fidel Castro Ruz. Fidel, born on August 13, 1926, was the son of Angel Castro, a Galician who came to Cuba in 1898 with the Spanish army, and Lina Ruz González, who entered the Castro household as a cook and became Angel's second wife. Fidel's father was grumpy and reserved, deeply marked by the harsh life of eastern Cuba. He managed

to make his fortune and found a prosperous agricultural business, with 500 employees, in Mayari. Fidel was sent to study with the Jesuits in Santiago and grew up to be athletic, bright, and eloquent. Then came July 26, 1953, which remains the historical date that changed both his and Cuba's destinies. That day, at dawn, 119 rebels launched an assault against the military barracks at Moncada in Santiago. Castro's five-hour speech before the courts became the ideological manifesto of the revolutionary movement, touching upon all the problems that afflicted his people: hunger, illiteracy, unemployment, prostitution, criminality, exploitation, and excessive foreign control

36 Fidel Castro was interrogated after the attack on the Moncada Barracks. On the left, Colonel Rio Chaviano was responsible for the torture and death of many prisoners. On the right, Lieutenant Pedro Sarria personally arrested Castro and saved him from death, first by removing him from a general execution and then placing him under arrest in a safe place.

36-37 On December 5, 1956, three days after the Granma landed in the swamp area of Las Coloradas, the guerrillas were heavily attacked by government troops at Alegria de Pio. After having to make a long and hard escape, the survivors, though exhausted, met on December 18 at Cinco Palmas, from where they regrouped to continue the fight.

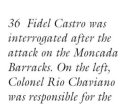

over wealth and means of production. Condemned to 15 years in prison, Castro was granted amnesty and released on May 15, 1955 because Batista, after the fraudulent elections of 1954, wanted to demonstrate a more moderate stance. Fidel left for Mexico, where he organized the men who were to fight in the revolution. He was joined by an Argentinean doctor who already had experience fighting in Guatemala: Ernesto "Che" Guevara. On November 30, 1956, while the leaders Haydée Santamaria, Celia Sánchez, Lester Rodríguez, and Vilma Espín led the revolt of Santiago, the *Granma*,

the yacht purchased by Castro, sailed with 82 armed men for the Cuban coast. The poorly coordinated insurrection failed, with the revolutionaries sustaining heavy losses, but Castro and the other survivors managed to save themselves thanks to the help of the people in the countryside. Declared dead by Batista, Castro meanwhile regrouped the guerrilla forces together with his brother Raul and, despite harsh police repression, made his first successful strike on January 17, 1957 with the attack on the La Plata Barracks, thus furnishing the rebels with a fresh arms supply.

37 top The long marches in the Sierra were hard due to hunger, horrible environmental and weather conditions, enemy attacks, and epidemics. With captured prisoners, the guerrillas adopted a specific line of conduct: they cured them and, in many cases, set them free.

37 bottom Che Guevara, with Fidel at his side, argues with a soldier. Born on June 14, 1928 in Rosario de Santa Fé, Argentina, Ernesto Guevara de La Serna lived as an anti-Peron exile, traveling through a large part of his continent. He met Fidel Castro in Mexico, thus beginning his Cuban adventure.

38 *Fidel Castro, leading a column of guerrillas, enters Havana. After having occupied Santiago on January 1 and leaving the command of the troops in the eastern sector to his brother Raul, Castro crossed the country, slowed by the rejoicing crowds.*

39 *Castro speaks to sugar-cane workers on August 11, 1960. A bitter war was fought to gain control of sugar production. On one hand, the United States stopped buying Cuban produce and supplying machinery; on the other, agrarian reforms hit American land holdings hard.*

40 left *The revolution, born with an openly patriotic and anti-colonialist attitude, only assumed a Communist and pro-Soviet-Union nature later on. Fidel Castro soon became the symbol and leader of the Cuban revolutionary and political process.*

40 right *In this 1960s Soviet postcard, a young Castro poses in front of the Cuban flag. A peculiar feature of Cuba communism is that it is prohibited to raise monuments to living people, therefore no statues of or squares named after the super-leader exist.*

41 *"On my island, inspired by their example, we will form our conscience and foster Communism," states the propagandist poster. Portraits of Castro and Guevara are always placed together with those of the fathers of the homeland, symbolic of perfect ideological continuity over the course of history.*

On February 17, 1957, the journalist Herbert L. Matthews of the *New York Times* reached Castro's encampment in the Sierra Maestra jungle and interviewed the leader. A week later, his paper published photographs from and an article about the meeting. Reactions in Cuba and the United States were very powerful. On March 13, a group of 76 men, of whom many were Catholics, attacked the presidential palace where Batista resided with the intent to kill the dictator, while another group interrupted Radio Reloj to read a revolutionary statement. The Batista administration responded with indiscriminate repressions, but showed itself to be unable to compete on a political level. On September 5, 1957, about 400 sailors, officers, and civilians occupied the Cienfuegos naval base, distributed weapons to the public, and battled Batista's army, which had to resort to calling upon the B26 bombers furnished by the United States under the joint U.S.-Cuba accord. In fact, the United States thereafter dampened relations with Batista because of his use of such brutal methods. Guerrilla warfare continued to expand its range over the territory, and on February 24, 1958, Radio Rebelde, the rebels' information outlet, began to transmit across the entire island. On November 30, the column led by Castro conquered the city of Guisa, and on December 30, Santa Clara fell, taken by the group led by Guevara. On December 31, the revolutionaries entered Santiago, and on January 1, 1959, Batista escaped to the Dominican Republic. On January 5, Manuel Urrutia, the judge who had defended the Moncada Barracks attackers, assumed the presidency of Cuba, and on February 16, Fidel Castro was nominated prime minister.

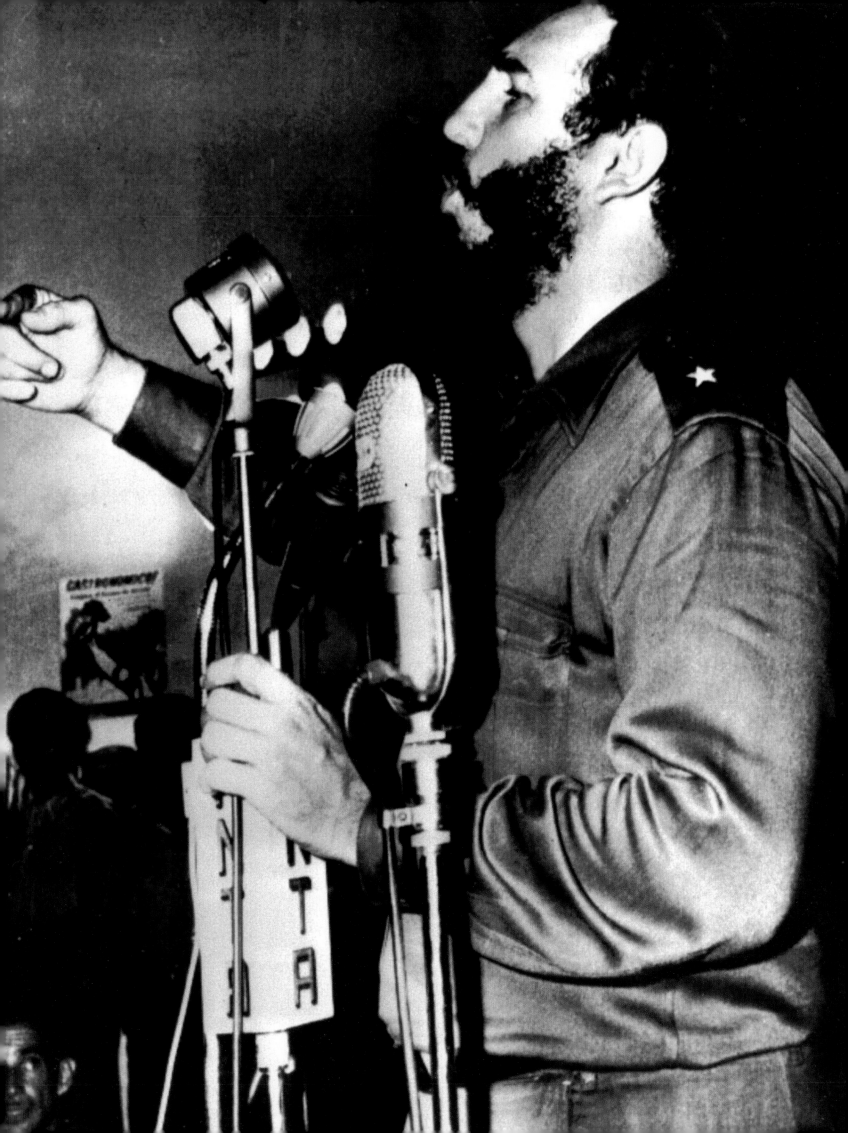

TODOS EN LA OFENSIVA REVOLUCIONARIA JUNTO A FIDEL

VIVA CUBA

EN MI ISLA

INSPIRADOS EN SU
EJEMPLO
FORMAREMOS
NUESTRA CONCIENCIA
Y CONSTRUIREMOS
EL COMUNISMO

42 top April 17, 1961: Cuban militiamen go to the Bay of Pigs to reinforce their defenses. In 72 hours, the battle finished with the disgraceful undoing of the anti-Castro faction and the embarrassment of the United States government, which was unable to hide its involvement in the preparation and execution of the attack.

42-43 President John Fitzgerald Kennedy, before a gathering of 40,000 anti-Castro Americans and Cubans, shows photographers the combat flag of a Cuban assault brigade that will take part in the attack in the Bay of Pigs. Amid the applause, he stated "I can assure you that this flag will be returned to this brigade in a free Havana."

Over the course of 1959, agricultural holdings larger than 1,000 acres were nationalized; almost all of them belonged to an American corporation, the United Fruit Company. Thousands of landowners, managers, and professionals moved to Miami, where they waited for things to change and for the Castro government to give them their properties back.

Counter-revolutionary groups supported by the CIA with the task of destabilizing the country and eliminating Castro started to operate. When in June 1960 the Texaco, Standard Oil, and Shell companies refuse

to refine crude oil from the U.S.S.R., the Cuban government decided to nationalize them. On June 6, 1960, President Eisenhower cut sugar imports from Cuba by 770,000 tons. It was the Cold War era, and every move by the United States against the Castro government pushed Cuba closer to the U.S.S.R. In fact, Moscow offered to buy Cuban sugar and to replace the techni-

cians who had left the country. In July, the Castro administration nationalized the telephone and electricity systems and confiscated $800 million in assets belonging to the United States. In January 1961, Castro ordered that the 300 employees of the United States embassy in Havana be reduced to 11, the same number of staff members at the Cuban embassy in Washington. The United States broke off diplomatic relations with Havana, prohibited its citizens from traveling to Cuba, and began the economic boycott of the island. On April 15, 1961, a force of 1,400 Cuban

political refugees trained by the CIA in Florida and Guatemala landed at Playa Girón, Playa Larga, and Bahía de Cochinos (Bay of Pigs), backed by B26 fighter planes sent by the Nicaraguan dictator Luis Somoza and the United States fleet. Despite heavy bombing by the B26s, the invading forces were brutally defeated by the Popular Militia led by Castro. The 1,197 prisoners they took were ransomed; the Kennedy Administration redeemed them with $53 million in medicine and food. On May 1, 1961, Castro announced the socialist nature of the Cuban revolution. Eighteen months later, on October 22, 1962, American planes discovered the launching pads of 42 Soviet nuclear missiles aimed at the United States and ordered their immediate dismantlement. A new world war seemed imminent, but on October 28, Khrushchev granted the American request. On October 9, 1967, Che Guevara was captured and killed in Bolivia where he had gone to activate revolutionary guerrilla warfare.

43 top left Cuban soldiers and militiamen test a piece of artillery used in 1961 in the Bay of Pigs. The landing of the anti-Castro fighters convinced the Cuban people of the necessity to strengthen their defenses, pushing them to permanent mobilization and alliance with the U.S.S.R. in order to procure an arms supply.

43 top right September 28, 1962: containers of IL-28 missile fuselages sail toward Cuba aboard the Soviet cargo ship Kasimov, in a photo shot from American planes. Castro asked for short-range missiles able to hit Miami, but Khrushchev decided to install missiles capable of hitting any point within the United States.

43 bottom left Castro and Khrushchev meet in New York in 1960, at the 15th session of the General Assembly of the United Nations. The alliance with the U.S.S.R. alarms Cubans in the political sector, who fear for civil liberties in their country.

44 bottom The
military parade of
January 2, 1979
celebrated the 20th
anniversary of the
revolution. The 1970s,
at the height of the

Cold War, saw the
"Brezhnevization"
of Cuban political
trends and a vigorous
ideological alignment
with Communist
principles.

44 top Fidel Castro,
photographed on June
23, 1977. On the
subject of Cuba, many
political observers
maintain that it is not
so much characterized
by Communism, but
rather "Fidelism."
Despite many attempts
on his life, Castro has
survived all of his
enemies.

In the 1970s, Cuba extended nation-alization to include the smaller land hold-ings, prohibited private commerce, and tightened relations even further with the U.S.S.R., which from 1973 on provided massive aid to the island's economy. The Cuban army intervened in Angola to back Agostinho Neto's M.P.L.A. against South Africa and its apartheid policies, and in Ethiopia, it provided support to the pro-Soviet leader Mariam Haile

Mengistu. After the collapse of the U.S.S.R. in 1989, the Cuban economy crashed and the new policies moved to-ward opening up to tourism and the pri-vate agricultural market. Three currencies were circulating on the island: Cuban pe-sos, exchangeable pesos, and American dollars. Now the Euro has joined them. The United States, first with the Torricelli Law and then with the Helms/Burton Act, tightened the boycott against the is-land. In August 1994, after waves of ille-gal emigrants fled to the United States, Castro allowed 35,000 Cubans to leave the island, and President Clinton, in 1997, arranged for 20,000 visas to be made available for Cubans wishing to move to America; applications numbered 435,000 and those to whom the visas were granted were chosen at random. Pope John Paul II visited Cuba from Jan-uary 21 to 25 in 1998, during which time he met with President Castro and called for the end of the "unjust and morally un-acceptable" American embargo. At that time, 11 million Cubans lived on the is-land and 1.5 million in the United States, 700,000 of whom settled in South Flori-da. In November 2000, George W. Bush was elected President of the United States, thanks partially to the determining vote of the anti-Castro Cubans in Miami.

44-45 Fidel Castro
and Pope John Paul
II meet on January
22, 1998 in Havana.
The pope's visit
revived freedom of
religion on the
island. The magazine

Juventud Rebelde, an
organ of the young
Communists, spoke of
a new alliance
between Catholics and
Communists against
the temptations of neo-liberalism.

45 bottom Castro speaks in the Karl Marx Theater in Havana on October 9, 2003, at the inauguration of the Salvador Allende School. Over the course of that same year, the Commission for Human Rights of the United Nations Organization asked to visit Cuba in order to check the living conditions of dissidents in prison.

THE SURREAL METROPOLIS

46 top left The buildings that face onto the Malecon exhibit the typically eclectic architectural style of Havana. Rafael Acosta wrote that the Malecon was the meeting point for the city, the sky, and the world.

46 top right The façade of the parish church sticks up from the square of walls surrounding the castle of San Carlos de La Cabaña, taken on the night of January 2, 1959 by Ernesto Che Guevara. With him, 400 guerrillas were on duty to watch over the city from the bastions.

46-47 The castle of El Morro, seen here from the Malecon, was built along the natural line of the rocks and in the shape of an irregular polygon to guard Havana's port. On the left, the lighthouse of El Morro, the oldest in Cuba, was built in 1845. Just under 160 feet tall, it offers a view that ranges over a distance of 43.5 nautical miles.

Havana, with 2.5 inhabitants, is Cuba's capital and the largest city in the Caribbean. Few cities in the world touch the heart like Havana. Few can elude the tourists' understanding with so much class. Havana is, in fact, a mosaic of intellectual and spiritual outlooks, of professions and trades, and of different human stories that twist and turn into a maze of contradictions. The city's foundation in 1514 under the name of San Cristóbal de La Habana, is tied to its fantastic position on a sheltered bay that made Cuba the "key" to the Americas. For centuries, all Spanish ships sailing to the colonies docked in the city's harbor. Buccaneers and pirates constantly threatened Havana. In 1555, it was sacked and burned by the French pirate Jacques de Sores. To defend the city, the Castillo de la Real Fuerza was erected, situated between the sea and the Plaza de Armas, where the military garrisons lived and trained. The building seems to be of medieval origin, with its wide moat, drawbridge, and robust bastions. One of the city's best loved symbols stands upon it: the statue of the Giraldilla, sculpted in 1630. It is a figure of a woman watching over the city, with her attentive gaze staring out to the horizon. She is believed to represent Isabel de Bobadilla, who waited in vain for the return of her husband, the governor Hernando de Soto, who disappeared during a military expedition in Florida in 1539. Isabel died of a broken heart. Between 1589 and 1610, the castle of the Three Kings of El Morro was built by the Italian Gian Battista Antonelli in a polygonal shape, with abundant cisterns and big enough to withstand a long siege. In 1630, the Punta Fort was erected to oversee the entrance to the bay from a high vantage point and armed with cannons. Havana thus became the best-protected city in all the Spanish colonies. Commerce in slaves, gold, marble, precious woods, textiles, fruit, tobacco, arms, sugar, rum, and coffee prospered. Following the English occupation of 1763, the Spanish built the impressive fortress of San Carlo de La Cabaña, completed in 1774.

48 top left The Real Fabrica de Tabacos La Corona was founded in 1845 in Calle Industria, a street in the center of the city behind the Capitol, by the Spaniard Jaime Partagas. One of the best tobacco factories in the country, it still employs 400 workers and produces such famous cigars as Churchills and Lusitanias.

48 top right A sequence of porticoes lines the Paseo de Martí near the Palacio de Los Matrimonios. Dating back to 1914, the neoclassical building is used for wedding ceremonies and civil functions. On Saturday mornings, young newlywed couples can be seen strolling beneath the porticoes.

48-49 The Paseo de Martí, more commonly known as Paseo del Prado, seen from the top of the Grand Theater. On the left, the white outline of the Cinema Peyret can be seen standing next to the Parque Central. Paseo de Martí crosses the center of the city from north to south.

With urban expansion, many dwellings were built outside the perimeter of the castles, creating the division between Old Havana and the new neighborhoods. In the early years of the 1800s, the city had a population of about 44,000 inhabitants, of whom 26,000 were blacks or mulattos; by the beginning of the 1900s, the number had grown to 240,000. The main urban center is divided into three parts: Central Havana, Old Havana, and Vedado. From the terrace of the Hotel Sevilla, where Graham Greene set *Our Man in Havana*, visitors can take in the impressive spread of concrete, rendered shinier and softer by the tropical blue of the sea and sky, and the layering of styles ranging from colonial architecture to early-1900s buildings, from socialist "citadels" to skyscrapers built with Soviet reinforced cement. The heart of the city beats in the downtown working-class neighborhoods, where the 1950s automobiles and old jalopies are more numerous and the everyday hustle and bustle is greater. On the grandiose Paseo de Martí, an avenue built in various stages between 1770 and 1928, school children wearing uniforms play with their teachers as the crowds stroll by or stop for a quick break on the marble benches. From there, the visitor can take the city's busiest pedestrian street, Calle San Rafael, located near the Hotel Inglaterra, a lovely colonial building where, in 1879, José Martí gave his famous speech on Cuban independence and, in 1898, the American journalists covering the Spanish-American conflict stayed.

49 top On Paseo de Martí, Hotel Inglaterra, built in 1875, is one of the oldest hotels in Cuba, with salons featuring colonial-era majolica tiling and furnishings from periods varying from the late 19th century to the 1950s. Some of its more illustrious guests included Sarah Bernhart, Federico Garcia Lorca, and Antonio Maceo.

49 bottom The 1905 statue of José Martí is located in the middle of the Parque Central, the square that links Old Havana to the downtown area. According to an old tradition, each day baseball fans gather here to enjoy heated discussions about their favorite teams.

Not far from the area stands the massive white structure of the Capitolio, built between 1929 and 1932, as ordered by the dictator Gerardo Machado. Headquarters of the Parliament until 1959, today it holds the Academy of Sciences and the National Library of Science and Technology. Inside, under its 203-foot-high dome, it contains a bronze of Jupiter that is considered the third-largest indoor statue in the world, and a copy of a 24-carat diamond. On the north side of the Capitol stands the Grand Theater of Havana, with 2,000 seats, since 1838 the headquarters of the Ballet Corps and the National Opera. In the vicinity is also the Museum of Fine Arts, featuring a superb collection of Cuban and European art, the Granma Pavilion, which shelters the yacht that brought Castro, Che Guevara, and their 80 companions back to Cuba, and the Museum of the Revolution. Walking along the east side of this last museum, the visitor reaches the church of Santo Angel Custodio, founded in 1687 by order of Archbishop Diego de Compostela, and rebuilt in 1871 in Neo-Gothic style. In José Martí was baptized in this church in 1853 and in its environs the writer Cirilo Villaverde set his famous novel *Cecilia Valdés*, the passionate story published in 1882 that meticulously describes the racial relations and daily life of the city.

50 top left The Capitol holds the masterpiece of Italian Angelo Zanelli: a bronze statue bathed in gold, which most likely portrays Minerva, weighs about 50 tons, and measures 46.5 feet tall.

50 top right The imposing staircase of the Capitol is decorated with six pairs of 46-foot-tall columns and two bronze statues, both the work of Italian Angelo Zanelli and symbolizing work and virtue.

50 bottom The internal vault of the Capitol emphasizes the building's height of almost 300 feet. A popular saying in Havana affirms, "Anyone who does not visit the Capitol cannot say they've seen Havana."

50-51 On Paseo de Martí, the impressive and massive Capitol is an imitation of its counterpart in Washington, D.C., in the United States. To build it, 5,000 workers labored for three years, two months, and 20 days, starting in 1926.

51 top The chandeliers and furnishings in the National Library of Cuba, inside the Capitol, were made in Europe and imitate Italian models.

52 top In this view, the tower of the Hotel Plaza is flanked, in the background, by the dome of the Capitol. Old Havana is the biggest and best-preserved colonial-era historical city center in the world.

52 bottom left An elegant dome rises from the top of the ex-presidential palace, today the Museum of the Revolution. On March 13, 1957, the building, then the residence of Fulgencio Batista, was unsuccessfully attacked by a group of armed students.

52 center right The building and population density in Old Havana was extremely high during the periods of both Spanish and American domination. Batista fostered the plan to raze a part of the old city to the ground in order to build hotels, skyscrapers, and casinos.

52 bottom right The Column of the Passion, located in front of the Banco Nacional, is just one of the many monumental sculptures with which Old Havana is brimming, the legacy of colonial-era Spanish-Catholic culture.

53 The Grand Theater dominates the Paseo de Martí at the point of the Parque Central and is, along with the Amedeo Roldan Theater, the most important center for performances – at a consistently high level – of the National Ballet School.

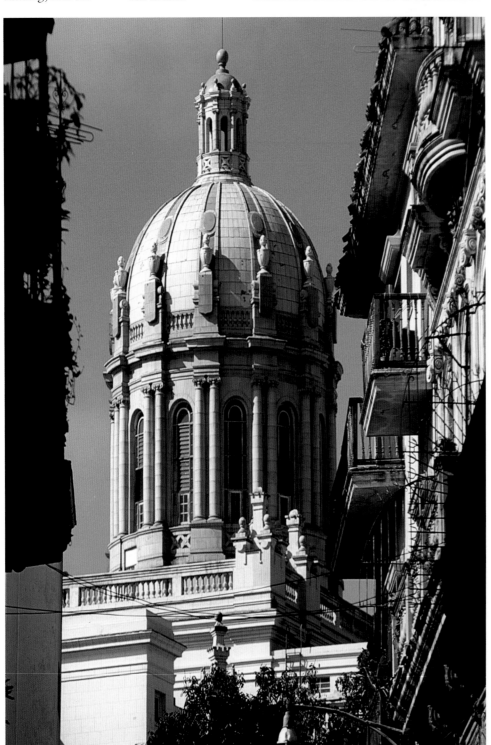

Taking Avenida de Italia, more commonly known as Galiano, the Malécon can be reached, the city's shore drive and symbol of its lifestyle. The construction of the Malécon, was begun by the American government in the early 1900s, and it extended from the Punta Fort to the monument in memory of the fallen of the battleship *Maine*. Forty years later, the work was extended a couple miles, as far as the Miramar neighborhood. A distinguishing characteristic of the Malécon is that not one single palm tree exists along the way. The presence of bars and shops is limited in some sections and the buildings, apart from the skyscrapers along the more modern extension, exhibit a mixture of styles, including the Baroque, Neo-Classical, Art Deco, Art Nouveau, and Modernist. The salty air has corroded the houses, once distinguished by shades of pink, brown, and sandy gray, and has transformed them into discolored skeletons. An important actor in the Malécon spectacle is the sea – not the calm version on hazy and breezeless days, but rather the furious one that on rainy days crashes against the wall, invades the street, and creates a whirlwind of colorful billows, shimmering sprays, and white fountains of light. Living on the Malécon on the ground floor means having the house flood several times a year, and decorating the apartment with things that hang a couple feet above the floor. However, people willingly put up with the inconvenience in exchange for the cool sea breeze that makes it possible to sleep on the hottest nights of summer. In the evening and at night, the shore drive comes alive with people playing instruments and dancing, chatting as they wait to be refreshed by a wave.

56 top left The spectacular space of the enchanting Old Square was used, in past centuries, as a market, for public functions and ceremonies, and for horse competitions, death sentences, and costume balls. Over time, the colonial aristocracy came to prefer it to the noisy Plaza de Armas,

always congested with maneuvering troops.

56 top right The slender outline of the Bacardi Palace from the early 1900s displays an eclectic interpretation of the Art-Nouveau style. Facundo Bacardi set up his first rum distillery in Santiago in the mid-1800s. His heirs, who left the

island after the 1959 revolution for the United States, took the brand name with them, which was replaced by another well-known label in Cuba.

56-57 A pretty clock stands out from the façade of a building near the Commerce Department, in the heart of Old Havana.

From the Malécon, it is possible to enter Old Havana. This is the city's oldest neighborhood, and in 1982 UNESCO designated it as a World Heritage Site. Thanks to international funding, part of the area has been restored, and can be seen today it all its glory: 16th-century streets, 17th-century Baroque churches, and fountains sculpted by great Italian masters. The rest of the neighborhood, is a working-class neighborhood with rickety houses and rundown facilities. The Old Square, founded in the 16th century, was the marketplace. It features perfectly preserved aristocratic residences dating from the subsequent centuries. Art galleries, photographic archives, and fashionable restaurants, located in old restored palatial homes, make Old Havana a sight to see for tourists.

57 bottom left Havana's charm does not reside only in its monuments, palaces, and churches, but also in the beauty of its urban fabric loaded with bits of art, sculpted spaces, and balconied windows, all

overlaid by the lines of a unique style.

57 top right From the ever-open windows and balconies of the old city, it is common to see women hanging their laundry.

57 bottom right The emblem painted on a majolica tile in an old street, in the heart of the old city, demonstrates the care the city's authorities are taking to restore Old Havana.

58-59 In Cuba, as an instrument of information and political propaganda, the mural is widely used. Instructors in what can be considered "on-street" art schools, the Cuban murals have become an important element in the island's panorama. In the photo, a detail from the big mural in Callejón de Jamel in Havana.

59 top left and right In these two vibrant views of Callejón de Jamel, not only is the expressive intention of the work evident, but also the salvaging of an otherwise deteriorated and insignificant urban landscape.

58 top "I can wait longer than you because I am time," reads the inscription on the mural in Callejón de Jamel, in downtown Havana. Considered art "by the masses and for the masses," or art in the service of the people, sometimes the murals also feature poetic expressions.

58 center Main characters in the murals are above all country folk and workers that are portrayed, often with stylized expressions clearly suggesting naivety, as they work or struggle against the enemy.

58 bottom Flying doves of peace form the background to the flow of pedestrians. Peace, war, independence, the revolution, the fathers of the homeland, Ernesto Che Guevara, and the fight against imperialism are constant themes in the murals of Cuba.

60 top left In Plaza de Armas, a used-book market functions, where it is possible to find old editions on Cuban history, biographies, the political essays of Fidel Castro and Che Guevara, and the first geographical and historical atlases of the revolutionary period.

60 top right The naïve paintings of country landscapes and reproductions of period automobiles are the best-selling subjects for the art dealers in Plaza de Armas. Every year, Cuba welcomes about a million tourists, each bringing in an income of about 1,500 dollars.

The cathedral of San Cristóbal, in Plaza de la Catedral, was completed in 1777, and is a hybrid of Colonial Baroque and 18th-century architectural styles framed by two bell-towers with different forms. Influenced by the style of the Italian school of Francesco Borromini, it was defined as "music transformed into stone" by the Cuban writer Alejo Carpentier. Inside, the sculptural pieces and gold work on the main altar, in Carrara marble, were done in Rome in 1820, and the three central frescoes were painted by the Italian painter Giuseppe Perovani. Facing onto the square are the mansion of the Marquis of Aguas Claras (today the restaurant El Patio) and the old residence of Don Luis Chacón. A few feet way, the famous bar and restaurant La Bodeguita del Medio used to boast a list of regular customers that included Ernest Hemingway, who from 1932 to 1939 stayed at the nearby Hotel Ambos Mundos, where it is possible to visit his room. A bronze statue of the writer leans, in the pose of a guest having a drink, on the Floridita bar, the place where every day Hemingway drank daiquirís, his favorite cocktail. To leave Old Havana, the visitor returns to the large Plaza de Armas, where El Templete stands, a small Neo-Classical chapel from 1828 that commemorates the place where, in the shade of a centuries-old ceiba tree, the first Mass was celebrated and the first governing body was set up in 1519. In the square – the oldest in the city – stand the Palacio de los Capitanes Generales and the Palacio del Segundo Cabo, or of the Vice Command, built starting in 1772 in a mixture of Baroque and Neo-classical styles with typical Andalusian elements. San Francisco Square, historically the second most important in the city, owes its name to the Franciscan convent built there in 1591. Today, it is dominated by the Commerce Department, built in Neo-Classical style beginning in 1909. The square looks like a typical Italian piazza with the "Lion Fountain" in the middle, a masterpiece from 1836 by the Italian Giuseppe Gaggini, who

60-61 In 1597, the square of the cathedral of Havana was crossed by the city's first aqueduct, which made the site unhealthy and humid. Thanks to the "builder" archbishop, Diego de Compostela, the area was reclaimed and rebuilt in the early years of the 18th century.

also sculpted the "India Fountain" in front of the Capitol. The church of San Francisco d'Assisi, founded in 1608 and rebuilt in 1738 in the Baroque style with a tall bell-tower, was deconsecrated in 1841 and today functions as a museum and a concert hall. The visitor wandering around Old Havana will see dozens of churches and stately buildings that make the city the most extraordinary example of colonial architecture in the world.

61 The Commerce Department (left) and the customs building of Havana's port dominate this view of San Francisco de Asís Square, framing the entrance to the harbor. The plaza is a spacious and elegant setting, connecting the marina to the old city.

62-63 In many Havana cafés, the myth of Ernest Hemingway, a big fan of Cuban cocktails, lingers in the air. The mojito, invented by Angel Martinez, was originally called a Drake because it is said that the admiral/pirate Francis Drake invented it. The drink is made with Cuban rum, lime, sugar, crushed ice, and mint leaves.

63 Opened by Angel Martinez at the end of the 1930s, the Bodeguita del Medio is famous for the quote attributed to Ernest Hemingway, "My mojito at the Bodeguita, my daiquirí at the Floridita." Hemingway's biographer, has stated that the phrase was just a publicity gimmick by Hemingway conceived to help his friend.

64 top Large porticoes lead to the Museum of the City of Havana, in the Palacio de los Capitanes Generales in Plaza de Armas. The original wood-plank walkways were replaced by cobblestone paving to reduce the noise made by marching troops.

64-65 The Museum of Colonial Art, in Plaza de la Catedral, is located in the house that belonged to Luis Chacón, built around 1720. The interiors are an example of the typical structure of houses of that era, with ceilings of wooden beams painted with the famous Havana blue, stained glass, Spanish-style furniture, and chandeliers of Murano glass.

65 top The restaurant El Patio, in the Plaza de la Catedral, occupies what was once the residence of the marquises of Aguas Claras. From the first floor, where typical Creole dishes can be tasted, a beautiful view of the square can be had.

65 bottom The Museum of the City of Havana, in Plaza de Armas, is located in Palacio de los Capitanes Generales. In its rooms, period furniture and carpets, Carrara marble bathtubs, and mirrors and chandeliers made in Venice can be admired.

66 *The best-known image of Ernesto Che Guevara in the world was reproduced on the building that, at the beginning of the Revolution, was the headquarters of the Ministry of Industry, directed by Che himself, and that today holds the Ministry of the Interior.*

67 *top left The famous monumental cemetery of Vedado contains the tombs of Cubans famous throughout the world, the martyrs of the wars of independence, and many revolutionaries. In the area, traffic is routed in such a way as to preserve the peace and quiet of the memorial park.*

67 *top right The monument to José Martí, the national hero of Cuba, dominates Revolution Square. The lookout at the top, at 466 feet high, is the highest point in the city and offers an interesting view of Havana.*

67 *bottom left The University of Havana features a solemn neoclassical entrance. Since 1959, over a half million students have graduated from the 47 university institutions in Cuba. Some 12,000 university teachers in 204 specialized centers participate in scientific research projects, but the collapse of the U.S.S.R has created difficulties in many sectors due to the lack of mechanical equipment.*

67 *bottom center This monument stands in a world apart from the universe of Havana's ordinary citizens, in Vedado, one of the city's most characteristic and sophisticated neighborhoods. The houses dating back to the early 1900s appear just as they were: the lack of resources prevents flashier renovations, but sometimes also means an accelerated rate of ruin for the dwellings.*

67 *bottom right The Ministry of the Interior, the focus of this panoramic view, and the Revolutionary Armed Forces constitute the armed defenses of present-day Cuban society. Every Cuban citizen must participate in the defense of his country by enlisting in the Militias of the Territorial Troops, where they learn to defend Cuba from enemy attack.*

Going around the center of the city from the west, the visitor reaches the Plaza de la Revolución, with its magnificent monument to José Martí, standing 466 feet tall on a star-shaped base and in front of which is the building housing the Central Committee of the Communist Party and the offices of Fidel Castro. Next to it, the Ministry of the Interior features an enormous mural portraying Che Guevara, with the words "Hasta la Victoria Siempre". From here, the visitor enters the Vedado neighborhood, which began to be developed in the early 1900s. One of the few houses built there before 1900 still stands, at the corner of Linea Street and Calle 2: a classic Spanish residence with a lovely internal courtyard; it was built in 1880. The neighborhood was inhabited by the upper class. The term Vedado derives from the Spanish word for forbidden, because access to the area, was prohibited to black people, who were heavily discriminated against at the time the first mansions were built in the 1900s. From the 1920s on, middle-class people also came to live in the Vedado neighborhood, and within a few decades, it became an elegant area full of diverse styles: Art Deco, Art Nouveau, Neo-Classical, and Modernist, with

houses embellished by verdant gardens and colonnades that allowed Havana to take the title of the city with the most columns in the world. The most luxurious development in the neighborhood is the monumental Cristóbal Colón Cemetery, opened in 1868. The park, with over 900,000 graves, contains the tombs of the Bacardi family, the Cuban chess player Raúl Capablanca, José Martí's mother, the fallen of the *Granma*,

Alejo Carpentier, and a lady, Amelia Goyri, who died in childbirth in 1901 and is especially idolized by many Cubans, who cover her tomb with flowers every day. Not far away, on Calle 17 in a public park, sits a lovely bronze statue of John Lennon on a bench by sculptor José Villa, commissioned and inaugurated on December 8, 2000 by the Cuban writer Abel Prieto, who also served as Minister of Culture.

68-69 The skyscrapers of Vedado face onto the Malecon. The most modern part of the neighborhood, with offices, shopping centers, hotels, these buildings with their square architectural style clash with the appearance of the rest of the residential area.

69 top Completed in 1930, the Hotel Nacional has been able to boast Winston

Churchill, Ava Gardner, and Frank Sinatra among its guests. In 1933, the building was the site of the attack of Batista's soldiers on Machado's men. Before the 1959 revolution, no black man or woman, of any nationality, was allowed to enter its premises.

69 center The salons of the Hotel Nacional feature drawings commemorating the

hotel's more famous guests, as well as photographic essays on the history of the Cuban revolution.

69 bottom The main hall of the Hotel Nacional, comes alive each evening with cabaret and music shows. Every day, the hotel hosts press conferences, and in autumn, it holds the Latin-American Cinema Festival.

The last jewel of Vedado, with a gorgeous view of the Malécon, is the Hotel Naciónal. UNESCO has designated it a World Heritage Site; in its lobby and restaurant it preserves intact the atmosphere of the era in which in was built: 1930.

Proceeding further west, the visitor enters the Miramar neighborhood, crossed by the most important avenue in the city, the Quinta Avenida, lined by tall trees surrounding embassies and banks. On the same avenue, also in a westerly direction, is Siboney, the residential area that, in the 1950s, replaced Vedado as the upper-class neighborhood, and, in Marina Hemingway, the tourist attraction port where the writer stayed when he took out his boat, the *Pilar*, for the annual marlin-fishing competition. Just outside the city, the Finca Vigía estate can be visited; Ernest Hemingway lived there from after World War II to 1960. His Royal typewriter is still on the table.

68 top left The Tropicana, an open-air club founded in 1939 in the Marianao neighborhood, features a 1950s-style variety show with over 200 dancers.

68 top right The table is set for breakfast at Finca Vigía, Ernest Hemingway's estate

seven miles from Havana. Three of the great writer's eight novels were set in Cuba: To Have and Have Not, The Old Man and the Sea, and Islands in the Stream. Of the others, two were set in Italy, two in Spain, and only one in the United States.

70-71 *The elegance of Santiago's architecture can be observed in this detail from a colonial-era building in the city center.*

71 *top left A collection of scores by Esteban Salas, the outstanding composer of choral and baroque music who arrived at Santiago in 1764, is preserved in the archives of the cathedral of Santiago de Cuba.*

70 *top The dome of the cathedral of Santiago de Cuba dates back to 1922, the year in which the last important restoration of the building was completed. It was erected in the first half of the 16th century and has frequently been damaged by earthquakes.*

70 *center The residence of Diego Velásquez, the oldest house in Santiago, had a gold smithy on the ground floor, evidence of what were, apart from declared purposes, the true intentions of Cuba's conquerors.*

70 *bottom The town hall of Santiago, a 1950s construction based on a 1783 design, is characterized by its tall central area with arched porticoes and long balconies. On January 1, 1959, from those balconies, Fidel Castro announced the victory of the revolution to the people of Santiago gathered in the square.*

A trip to Cuba could easily begin in the "Deep East," from its capital, Santiago. On the cultural level, this city of 440,000 inhabitants competes with Havana: it has a renowned university, and above all, was the cradle of the revolutionary movement that by the end of the 1950s changed the history of the island. In the past, it accepted numerous French colonists, ex-Haitian slaves, Catalan immigrants, Chinese, Dominicans, and Jamaicans, who joined the groups of people of Indian, African, and Spanish origin to create a lively combination of cultural identities and world views. Santiago is surrounded by mountains that have historically isolated it from the rest of Cuba while making it more open to the Caribbean cultures of nearby countries. It was founded in 1514 by Diego Velásquez, a few miles from the site selected in 1522, where it has developed until today. Capital of Cuba for a few decades, Santiago was unseated by Havana. It was sacked by the pirates Jacques de Sores in 1554 and Henry Morgan in 1662, and in 1675 was devastated by an earthquake. Santiago is the "blackest" city in Cuba: only one-fourth of the population is white; its other inhabitants are black or mulatto. A tour of the city, with its lovely colonial look, can start from Céspedes Park, the old Plaza de Armas, where a bronze bust commemorates the hero of the first Cuban war of independence. Looking onto the park, the house of Diego Velásquez, from 1522, originally had a gold foundry on the ground floor, with the private rooms on

the upper floors. Today, it holds an exhibit, in its beautiful period rooms, of furniture and objects from the 16th to the 19th centuries. On the south side of the square stands the imposing cathedral of Santiago, rebuilt in 1922 in an eclectic style. The interesting and lovely Carnival Museum illustrates the history of a ritual that in Santiago is sumptuously celebrated each year, beginning in mid-July and duly participated in by all Santiagoans.

71 top right In Revolution Square stands the grandiose monument to Antonio Maceo. The sculpture, the work of the Santiagoan Alberto Lescay, is about 53 feet tall, weighs over 120 tons, and is clad with 23 steel plates. The square has a surface area of 570,000 square feet and can hold 200,000 people.

72 top left In the cemetery of Santa Ifigenia, in Santiago de Cuba, the mausoleum of the "Apostle of the Independence," José Martí, occupies a central position. The island's poetic voice and author of famous hymns and compositions, Martí fell in combat on May 19, 1895 and was then moved to this city, a symbol of Cuban liberation.

72 top center The monument dedicated to the patriot Francisco Sanchez Echevarria stands in Plaza de Marte. In Cuban culture, Santiago is considered the city where the independence movement got started and, in the 1950s, which generated the revolutionary movement that lead to the seizing of power in 1959.

72 top right Plaza de Marte in Santiago was originally a Spanish parade ground, founded in 1800, where Cuban prisoners were led before firing squads.

72-73 A façade of the Don Martín del Cado rum factory recalls the origins of the spirit, invented in Martinique in the 17th century through the distillation of molasses syrup, the residue of sugarcane processing. In Cuba, rum is not only the main ingredient of countless cocktails, but it is also what Cubans drink with meals on holidays and days off.

Carnival is organized by various folkloristic groups (*comparsas*) such as Carabalí Izuama, Tumba Francesa, Carabalí Olugo, and the Conga de Los Hoyos. These were formed centuries ago and jealously preserve their customs, including the live music played by excellent performance groups, the clothing, the costumes, and the traditional dances. Music and dance can be observed and studied at the headquarters of the artistic groups. In 107 Calle Pio Rosada, one of the oldest Comparsas del Carnevale associations has its office: the Foco Cultural Carabalí Isuama, which studies the dances of *caribalí obulo*, *tumba francese*, and *conga*. In the House of Traditions, on Calle Rabí, the Foco Cultural El Tivolí performs the *orishas*, *bembé*, and *palo monte* religious dances. Extraordinary dance steps can also be seen on Saturdays at the Teatro Oriente, where the Ballet Folclorico Cutumba performs, a top-quality dance company that studies ancient dances like the *gagá*, the *columbia*, and the *tajona*. Continuing the tour of Santiago, the visitor reaches the Emilio Bacardi Museum, founded in 1899 by the well-known Cuban rum distiller. Then, there is the house of Antonio Maceo, the early-1800s residence where the heroic fighter for the freedom of Cuba was born. The last pearl in Santiago's string of sights to see is the castle of El Morro, designed in 1587 by the Italian Giovanni Battista Antonelli and built between 1633 and 1693. The castle is located in a pleasant position atop a high promontory, ad with its perfectly preserved storerooms, rooms, halls, and bastions, it was declared a World Heritage Site by UNESCO in 1997.

73 top A mural with the national colors white, red, and blue, features the faces, from left to right, of José Martí, Máximo Gómez, and Antonio Maceo, the three proud fighters of the independence movement.

73 bottom Young women and girls in Santiago get ready for the Carnival parade, which coincides with the 50th anniversary of the attack on the Moncada Barracks.

74 top left The cathedral of Our Lady of the Assumption in Baracoa, erected in 1833, holds the Parra cross, which, according to some sources, Columbus carried on his caravel during the 1492 voyage.

74 top right The fourth largest city in Cuba, Holguín, founded in 1523, is famous for brewing the best beer and making the most

highly-valued musical instruments on the island.

74-75 Coconut plantations and woods surround Baracoa, nestled comfortably on its bay. Northwest of the city runs the Toa River, the biggest in Cuba in terms of water capacity. In the Cuchillas de Toa area, the river is part of a biosphere reserve protected by UNESCO.

At the easternmost point off the island is Baracoa, the first city that the Spanish founded in Cuba. Diego Velásquez set up a stable governing body there in 1512. The town, with 50,000 inhabitants, is full of colonial traces and old Spanish forts, and is surrounded by dense forest. After a long journey across the lush green of the endless cultivated fields, another large city is reached: Holguín, with 240,000 inhabitants, where an organ factory can be visited and bands playing mechanical organs can be listened to. In the same province, near the village of Biran, is Finca Las Mañacas, the old estate of the Castro family. Returning south, the visitor enters the quiet town of Bayamo, with the gorgeous house of Carlo Manuel de Céspedes and walks through the pretty, tree-lined avenues.

75 top Baracoa honors Christopher Columbus with a monument by the sea. The navigator approached the local population with the offer of a compromise between the two parties, and for this reason, the Spanish ostracized him.

75 bottom Baracoa exudes history. Many of its old buildings, like this one in the photo or the Hotel La Rusa, built by Magdalena Rovieskuya, had such famous guests as Castro and Guevara, Errol Flynn, and Alejo Carpentier.

76 In the green countryside around Baracoa, coconut plantations and cocoa fields are taking over again. In Finca Duaba, the factory of the same name can be visited and it is possible to take a swim in the Duaba River and eat the typical and traditional dishes of the region.

77 top In all Cuban cities, in this case in Baracoa, playgrounds for children and well-equipped open green spaces are numerous. Many observations about Cuba speak of a "dignified poverty" to distinguish the Cuban phenomenon from the striking indigence that afflicts a large number of Latin-American peoples.

77 bottom Two children in Baracoa wearing school uniforms. The national literacy campaign has made it possible to overcome illiteracy, and rural programs of enrollment have made the right to an education accessible to every child. Where no schools exist, volunteers will travel to teach.

78-79 *Domed galleries and the bell tower of Our Lady of Mercy pop up among the roofs of the city of Camagüey.*

79 top *The church of the Holy Christ of Travels, from the early years of the 19th century, stands in Cemetery Square in Camagüey. The religious building exhibits typical* *features of Cuban baroque, with elements taken from several architectural traditions.*

79 center *Today a convent, the basilica of Our Lady of Mercy in Camagüey was built in 1748 and reconstructed in 1848. Inside, the building features a vault with baroque frescoes.*

79 bottom *In Ignacio Agramonte Park in Camagüey, once the Plaza de Armas, stands the monument dedicated to Ignacio Agramonte, a hero of the Cuban independence. The city also boasts a museum named after* *him, located in a barracks of the Spanish cavalry built in 1848, which contains collections of period artifacts, historical finds, late-19th-century paintings by Fidelio Ponce, and ancient urns.*

The third largest city in Cuba with 300,000 inhabitants, Camagüey (previously Santa María del Puerto Principe), is located further west. The city is made up of narrow, winding streets and elegant colonial buildings that hide adorable courtyards with luxuriant gardens. Plaza San Juan de Díos is dominated by the hospital of the same name, in operation until 1972 and today a nursing school, with its lovely cloister and charming treatment halls. Plaza del Carmen and Plaza de Armas offer fascinating and gracious glimpses of the past. Camagüey features many intact colonial-era houses representative of an adaptation of the ancient Roman house: they are surrounded by an external wall and endowed with an open courtyard in the middle of the house. This type of dwelling met both security requirements and the need to live in cool and shady spaces. The patio, often decorated in Moorish style, the legacy of the Arab tastes that had influenced Spain, became the social as well as physical hub of the house, and was embellished with works in marble and wrought iron that emphasized its function. Terraces and verandas abound, where it was possible to enjoy a cool breeze and escape the heat, and the roofs were usually in wood or terracotta tiles. Strategically placed below the gutters, there were always large jars that served to collect rainwater, hence the reason for which Camagüey is also known as the "city of jars."

Leaving Camagüey, the visitor travels across the pretty countryside of the Ciego de Avila province to reach some of the most pleasant seaside spots in Cuba.

80-81 and 81 top left Camagüey. Cars in the provincial cities are often antiques. In fact, modern means of transportation are found mainly in Havana, where the majority of diplomatic missions and offices of the departments of the Cuban state are located. In the 1950s, Cuba imported more Cadillacs than did many other parts of the world.

81 top right In a street in Camagüey, a man lugs a cart loaded with plantains, a type of banana that can be eaten in many ways, such as fried and salted, cooked with sugar, or when very ripe, stuffed with meat and baked. Cuban cuisine makes good use of the island's exceptional variety of fruit.

80 top In Camagüey, the use of wood in the balconies is characteristic. The city has grown continuously over recent decades, but the layout of the historical center has remained intact and reflects the wealth of the colonial era, when the people of Camagüey got rich by meat and leather smuggling.

80 center The white of the pilasters against backgrounds painted in "Havana blue" characterizes the entrance halls of many houses in Camagüey. Though this shade is the most commonly used in restorations, white, pink, pale yellow, dark saffron, light green, cream, dark blue, and sky blue are also widely used.

80 bottom A painter carries a painting through the streets of Camagüey. Cuba is experiencing a real boom in the arts. The Academy of San Alejandro and the many art schools train top-quality artists, whereas a slew of young self-taught artists produce naïve works for the tourist market.

82 bottom Though it has no colonial-era historical center, Ciego de Ávila is full of old buildings along its downtown streets.

82-83 In Moron, in the province of Ciego de Avila, a modern bronze sculpture, which "sings" at dawn and dusk, has led to the square being named Plaza of the Rooster.

83 top An electric-diesel engine enters the train station of Ciego de Ávila. Following the close-down of the railway in Jamaica in 1992, Cuba became the only Caribbean country to have a rail system. On the island, there are 7,598 miles of tracks, which are served by 285 steam locomotives used to transport sugar cane.

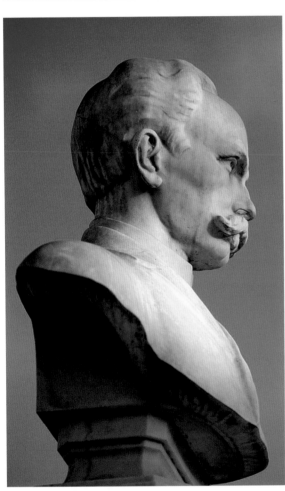

82 top In Ciego de Ávila, as in all the province, carriages are popular means of transport. The scarcity of buses has also led trucks being used as a means of public transport.

82 center left A 1925 bust honors the memory of José Marti in Ciego de Ávila. A factory manufactures thousands of these busts in the image of the "Apostle of the Cuban Independence."

82 center right The Bank of Credit and Commerce in Ciego de Ávila is a severe construction in neoclassical style. Until 1934, it only circulated American dollars. In 1934, the currency of the Republic of Cuba came into use, and in 1949, the currently used bills of the Banco Nacional de Cuba.

In the central region of the island, Santa Clara, with its 207,000 inhabitants, was founded in 1689 by a rich aristocrat looking to escape the pirate attacks taking place along the coastal regions. In Santa Clara, at the end of 1958, Ernesto Che Guevara led the attack on an armored train loaded with ammunition, arms, and soldiers. In Revolution Square stands the mausoleum, inaugurated by Fidel Castro on October 8, 1997, that holds the remains of Guevara and other revolutionaries killed in Bolivia in 1967 and later returned to Cuba.

86-87 The blue shade of an arcade enlivens a street in Placetas, in the province of Villa Clara. In cities with greater exposure to the midday sun, the colors chosen to paint the houses serve not only for esthetic purposes, but also to reduce the reflection of the sun.

87 top left Even Placetas has its own monument to José Martí. Besides fighting and dying for Cuba, the "Apostle of the Independence" fought for a new vision of Latin America that would give back to its inhabitants pride in their identity, finally free from all colonial influences. In Cuba, the monuments in his memory are countless.

87 top center The sculpted gateway of this old colonial building in Placetas, with an ornate lintel and decorative opening, displays an emphatic and carefully chosen design that is typical of Cuba.

87 top right The town hall in Placetas is in Neo-Classical style with pilasters and entablature emphasized by bright chromatic color combination.

86 top Chickens for sale at a stall in Placetas. A dollar-driven economy has supplanted that of the peso, and it is hard for Cubans, in modern-day island, to find businesses that sell products in the native currency at reasonable prices.

86 bottom A half-century-old automobile is parked in an improvised house "carporch" in Placetas. The old cars are passed down from generation to generation without, at least it would seem, any change in their motor functions. It is impossible to imagine the Cuban landscape without these cars.

88-89 Trinidad, in 1797, had reached such a high level of splendor as to be appointed the seat of government for the island's entire central territory.

89 top left In Trinidad, at the end of Plaza de Mayor, stands the church of the Holy Trinity, reconstructed in 1892 in one of the oldest places in the city.

Inside, the Christ of the True Cross, of 1793, is considered one of the most beautiful sculptures of Jesus Christ in Latin America.

89 top right The land in Los Ingenios Valley, marked by sugar-cane farms, features the very old buildings of farmhouses and distilleries.

Continuing on to the luxuriant Valley of Los Ingenios, in the middle of the incredibly green fields of sugar cane, the property of Pedro Iznaga can be seen. It dates from the second half of the 18th century, and still features the 144-foot tower from which slaves working the fields were overseen; there is also the house bell, rung to call them to the harvest. Lying beyond the charismatic ruins of the old sugar mills is Trinidad, a small city of 50,000 inhabitants that UNESCO designated a Heritage of Humanity site in 1988. The third Spanish settlement in chronological order after Baracoa and Bayamo, Trinidad was for centuries the heart of the smuggling traffic, dealing in slaves from Jamaica, tobacco, livestock, skins, and rum. At the beginning of the 19th century, thanks to the heavy immigration of French colonists fleeing Haiti, the Trinidad region succeeded in producing one-third of the Cuba's total production of sugar cane. The city embellished itself with squares, churches, and palatial buildings, testimony to the affluence achieved. Because of the wars of independence, crisis and ultimately decline followed. However, this meant that Trinidad was saved from the savage urbanization that spoiled other historical city centers in Cuba.

88 top The middle of Los Ingenios Valley is the site of the property of the powerful Iznaga family. This influential family lived in the second half of the 18th century. Slaves were called to work in the sugar-cane fields from its bell-tower.

88 bottom From the top of the convent's bell tower, Trinidad offers a pleasant view of its characteristic roofs, covered with local tiles, and internal courtyards, with their lush tropical vegetation.

90 top left In the small streets of Trinidad, smoothed cobblestone pavement, carts, carriages, and period automobiles, and low old houses are features of the enchanted atmosphere of one side of a modest lifestyle, which has fortunately been preserved for all to enjoy.

90 top right An automobile dating back to the early part of the 20th century that is so old-fashioned that it seems to be part of a movie. It is parked in front of a house in an alley in Trinidad. The lifestyle of the city has changed little over the last century.

90-91 Lively hues embellish Plaza Mayor, in Trindad. The esthetic budget of a city decorated in deep colors, in greens, white, and yellows, is combined with a simple beauty featuring wrought iron painted in white in the shapes of flowers, arabesques, vases, rose windows, and peacock tails.

The city is not much different from the description written by Alexander Friedrich von Humboldt, the German naturalist and traveler who wrote an essay on Cuba in 1826. To ensure a leisurely exploration of Trinidad's historical center, the visitor can stay in one of the old period houses. The town history museum is an aristocratic mansion: from its tower, a view of the entire city can be enjoyed. The parish church of the Holy Trinity, in Plaza Mayor, exhibits its Neo-Classical appearance, while standing next to it is the Brunet Building – now the Museum of the Romantic Era – the splendid residence of the family of Count Brunet with Empire-style furnishings, canopy beds, Bohemian-crystal chandeliers, and a collection of antiques and 19th-century canvases painted by the Cuban painter Esteban Chartrand.

91 top The pleasing vertical thrust of the bell tower of the Holy Trinity in Trinidad competes with the soaring trunk of a royal palm tree.

91 bottom left The church of the Holy Trinity overlooks the courtyard of the Museum of Architecture, with its arcade covered in locally made terracotta tiles. In a late-18th-century setting, the museum holds architectural models of colonial-era patrician residences.

91 bottom right Plaza Mayor in Trinidad flaunts its rich, lavish, and fairy-tale-like decoration, carefully designed down to the smallest details. Part of the paving stones in this famous square is in chinas pelonas, meaning smooth stones from a riverbed.

92 top left The inside of a house in Trinidad features oils on canvas from the second half of the 19th century as well as religious symbols kept in a wooden tabernacle.

92 top right Trinidad's Historical Museum was the residence of a rich family. Decorated in neoclassical style, it contains well-preserved colonial-era furnishings.

92 bottom Brunet Manor, or the Museum of the Romantic Age, is a rare example of a two-story building in a city where almost all the houses are low. In the building, it is possible to visit 13 rooms and the internal courtyard. The central entrance staircase and the ceilings are in mohagany, the floors in marble, the furniture in English Empire style, and the chandeliers in Bohemian crystal.

92-93 The splendor of this room, in a house in Trinidad, recalls the opulence of the colonial nobility. Tourism has had a notable impact on the peace and quiet of city life, but Trinidad seems to have maintained an atmosphere of the olden days.

93 top In a house in Trinidad, the statue of a Roman soldier with a Christian cross in its hand stands next to a dresser dating back to the mid-1800s, on which period silver is displayed.

94 top In Sancti
Spíritus, the Puente
Yayabo, a bridge over
the river of the same
name, is a national
monument of the
island. Legend has it
that the clay used in
its construction, in
1815, was mixed with
goat's milk.

94 bottom left
Sancti Spíritus,
founded in 1514, is
located at the
geographical center of
Cuba and is the oldest

city in the island's
interior. Though
sacked by pirates
in 1665, it grew
thanks to trade in
agricultural products.

94 bottom right With
a marble sculptural
group, Sancti Spíritus
honors its citizen
Serafín Sanchez, a
patriot who
participated in both
the wars of
independence and
died in battle in
November 1896.

Continuing on to Sancti Spíritus, the
visitor comes to the Puente Yayabo, a
brick bridge built in 1815 in front of the
1876 Teatro Principal. In Cienfuegos and
Remedios, enchanting colonial-era cities,
time seems to stand still. In Matanzas, in a
gorgeous location on the north coast,
some of Cuba's treasures can be visited:
Teatro Sauto, from 1862, where the famous Italian tenor Enrico Caruso per-
formed; the well-preserved Triolett phar-
macy, founded in 1822; and Vigía Editions, which publishes handmade books
that are true collectors' items.

94-95 Two
schoolchildren in
Sancti Spíritus leave
for class. The
education system in
Cuba is comparable
to that of some of the
richest countries in
the world, and there
are laws preventing
the exploitation of
child labor.

95 top left A calash
crosses a street in
Sancti Spíritus, in
which the geometric
designs in ivory
yellow and sky blue
blend with the lines of
the wrought-iron
work on the windows.

95 top right A state
employee walks on
the stone paving of a
deserted street. In
Sancti Spíritus, there
are no tourists and
there is absolute
peace and quiet in
the city.

96-97 *José Martí Park, in Cienfuegos, contains a monument to the "Apostle" of the liberation of Cuba. In the foreground, on the left, part of the arch commemorating the triumph of independence, dating back to 1902, can be seen. The cathedral rises in the background.*

96 bottom *In Cienfuegos, Palacio del Valle features an eclectic Neo-Moorish architectural style. It was built as a private residence in 1917, and today is a famous restaurant. Skilled Moroccan laborers participated in its construction.*

97 top Government Hall faces the south side of José Martí Park in Cienfuegos. The building was the seat of colonial administration since its foundation, in 1819, and today contains the offices of the Poder Popular Provinciale.

97 bottom left Cienfuegos was originally inhabited by French colonists and developed upon the arrival of the railroad, in 1850, which brought the city travelers en route to Santiago. Today, it has become an important hub for fishing and industry.

97 bottom right Made pleasantly genteel by delicately contrasting hues, a neoclassical façade looks onto José Martí Park in Cienfuegos. Thanks to the refined style of its buildings, the city has been given the nickname of the "Paris of Cuba."

98 top A folklore group performs Afro-Cuban dances in Matanzas province. The culture, music, and traditional dances of Cuba's black population are experiencing great success, accompanied by the gradual reverse of racist mentalities on the island.

98 bottom and 99 In Varadero, in Matanzas province, remarkable tourist resorts are being developed. The largest seaside resort in the Caribbean is being built there, boasting 15 miles of white beaches, according to information provided by the travel agencies. Cuba expects to soon attract more than two million tourists a year.

A NATURAL ENVIRONMENT WORTH SAVING

100 top left The Cuban coasts, on the north side, are cooled by trade winds blowing from the northeast in winter and from east-northeast in summer. In October, the island may often be hit by squalls and hurricanes.

100 bottom left The waves of the sea crash against a rocky tract of coastline in the

Holguín area. In Cuba, the wind is a climatic constant that mitigates the tropical heat.

100 right The coast of Jibacoa, in Havana province, is about 40 miles from the capital. The region is characterized by tall limestone cliffs and clear, clean water good for snorkeling.

The island of Cuba, in the Caribbean Sea, is 39,385 square miles in area. From east to west, it is 775 miles long. At its narrowest point, at the bay of Mariel, it is only 19 miles from coast to coast; at its widest, between the north coast of Camagüey and Camaron Grande Point, it is 118 miles wide. The total length of Cuba's indented coastline is 3,563 miles, 1,990 along the north coast and 1,573 on the south side. The second largest island in the Cuban archipelago is the Isle of Youth (849 square miles), followed by Cayo Romano and Cayo Coco (358 and 143 square miles, respectively). Cuba's climate is humid and tropical, but thanks to its thin and elongated shape, the weather is mitigated by the sea and the trade winds that blow along the coast from the northeast. Cuba's 4,194 islands are gathered in vast archipelagoes. The

101 Swelling breakers assault the coast near Playa Juragua, in Santiago de Cuba province. Situated between the Gulf of Mexico and the Caribbean Sea, in the heart of the American Mediterranean, Cuba offers visitors an abundant variety of marine settings.

archipelago of Los Canarreos, northeast of the Isle of Youth, contains 672 *cayos* and *cayuelos*, islands and islets surrounded by a crystalline sea. The Jardines de la Reina Archipelago, south of the Camagüey coast, has 662 islands, many of which are tiny, forming a maze that is nearly impossible to navigate, set in a sea that makes for a stunning background. The ocean environment is, generally, uncontaminated, and some Cuban beaches are considered among the most beautiful

102-103 The bright turquoise color is dazzling in this view of a lagoon in the area of Playa Girón, in Matanzas province. After the fall of the U.S.S.R., tourism became the base of the Cuban economy.

in the world. The coral reefs are numerous and hide an underwater treasure chest of sea life, both animal and plant. Tours can begin by traveling the most magnificent coastal road in Cuba toward Marea del Portillo, in the eastern province, where an enchanting mile-long black-sand beach awaits visitors. It is also interesting to visit the Sierra Maestra, with its lovely mountain habitat and historical sites commemorating the revolutionary guerrilla war. The Sierra boasts the tallest mountains on Cuba: the Turquino (6,477 ft) and Cuba Peak (5,939 ft).

It is possible to reach the American base at Guantanamo and, accompanied by a Cuban guide, get a peek at it from the top of a hill. Between Santiago and the Baconao River, extends Baconao Park, a UNESCO -designated biosphere reserve, with its gorgeous, pristine rocky coastline populated by beach crabs. Not to be missed are the panoramic route to the Punta Maisí lighthouse, at the easternmost point of the island, and, northeast of Holguín, the two-mile-long Guardalavaca Beach, with its spectacular coral reef and a sea floor of rare beauty.

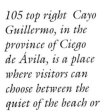

On the southern coast, mangroves host dense colonies of pink flamingos and pelicans and the reef provides a rich marine background. In *Islands in the Stream*, Ernest Hemingway wrote about these places, where he loved to fish from his boat, and which are still enthralling today. South of the Ciego de Ávila and Camagüey coast, the Jardines de la Reina Archipelago is a paradise of mangroves and perfectly intact deep coral banks. Here, the *macabi*, commonly known as the bonefish, is still a draw, a legendary creature well known to all fishing enthusiasts with strong enough lines to fight it. Back in Cuba's central region, Cayo Santa María can be visited, where a 30-mile-long raised road leads to an immense beach of white coralline sand. In Varadero, an internationally famous seaside spot since the beginning of the 1900s, deep-sea fishing, golf, and parachuting can be enjoyed. In the central region, to the south, visitors can stay on the beautiful beaches of the Ancón Peninsula or breathe the cool air of the tall mountain at Topes de Collantes. In Pinar del Río, the westernmost province of the country, fabulous scuba diving can be done at María la Gorda and Cayo Levisa. In the Los Canarreos Archipelago are the paradises of Playa Sirena and Cayo Largo del Sur, where the sea water takes on the colors of the underwater coral, and the beaches, shimmering with mother of pearl, feature turtles, iguanas, and pelicans. Coralline beaches lapped by a crystal clean sea are not lacking on the nearby Isle of Youth either.

108 and 109 Every shade of blue and turquoise can be seen in this photo of Cayo Coco, seen from above. Cayo Coco is located 250 miles south of Nassau in the Bahamas. The island, with 140 square miles, opens on its north side with a beach of six miles of the whitest sand, whereas the more humid southern coast of the cayo is covered by mangroves. Since 1988, Cayo Coco has been connected to the mainland by a road running over an artificial jetty that cuts the island's glass-like sea in two, affecting the dolphin population, which can no longer circle the island, and the cormorants, pelicans, and flamingos, for which reproduction rates are falling.

110 top This series
of sinuous basins
belongs to a complex
of swimming pools
of a vacation resort
in Cayo Coco.

110-111 The
northeastern zone of
Cayo Coco is
undergoing constant
development, in
response to the ever-
increasing demands
of tourism in Cuba.

111 top left Lined by
bright white yachts, a
pier extends from a
resort in Cayo Coco.
In this famous spot,
there are excellent
facilities for
yachting, fishing,
and all kinds of
underwater sports.

111 top right In
Cayo Coco, the
shadow of a tourist
plane is outlined
against the edge of
a pool of brackish
water, which winds
around the back of
a residential area.

*111 center In Cayo
Coco, visitors can
try deep-sea fishing.
The legendary
marlin, swordfish,
tarpon, sawfish,
yellowfin tuna,
dolphin fish, and
mako (a 13-foot
shark with a blue
back) can be caught.*

*111 bottom Lonely
chaises longues face
the horizon and the
sea, along a strip of
beach on Cayo Coco.*

112 and 113 These aerial views show the dense vegetation found on Cayo Coco and the road that crosses the island. *For unstated reasons, both this location and Varadero are forbidden to Cuban citizens. Only Cubans who work in the resorts can enter the area, and only for the time necessary to do their jobs. Whereas many consider Cayo Coco a vacation paradise on the sea, others believe it is a place reserved just for foreign tourists, completely unreflective of the reality of life on Cuba.*

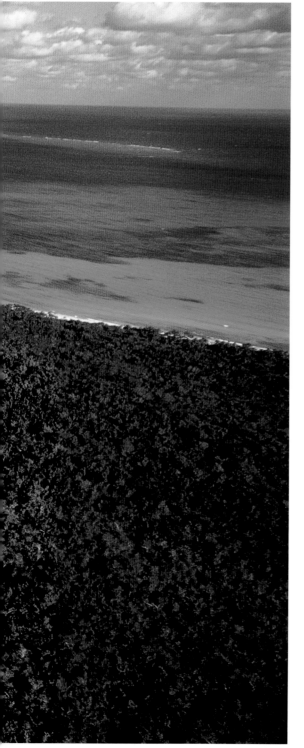

114 top A cone-shaped mogote interrupts the flat farmed fields in Viñales. These calcareous formations date back to the lower- or mid-Jurassic period.

114 center The Viñales Valley is squeezed to the north by the Guaniguanico Cordillera, which includes the Sierra del Rosario, cloaked by forests.

114 bottom In a perspective dominated by far-off mogotes, the rows of tobacco plants seem to extend infinitely across the Viñales Valley.

114-115 In the Viñales Valley, including the province of Pinar del Río, the countryside features idyllic peace and quiet. In the background rise mogotes.

Cuba's interior, originally covered by centuries-old forests, has been greatly changed by agricultural expansion and is characterized overall by the vast expanses of sugar-cane plantations, whose produce constitutes 50 percent of the country's exports. Fields of tobacco, coffee, cocoa, and citrus and other fruits also contribute to the colors of the Cuban landscape. One fourth of the Cuban territory is mountainous. Located in the middle of the island, the Guamuhaya Sierra rises to 3,740 feet with the peak of San Juan. To the west, in Pinar del Río region, in the plain where the florid tobacco crops stand tall before being harvested to make the world's best cigars, the *mogotes* pop up, round hills that are the result of thousands of years of erosion. Of Cuba's total territory, 19 percent is occupied by forest (in 1812, it was 90 percent; in 1900, 54 percent; and in 1959, before the revolution, it was 14 percent). The wooded area is prevalently composed of semi-deciduous species smaller than evergreens.

115 top left Sugar cane is blooming in the province of Sancti Spíritus. Christopher Columbus introduced this crop to Cuba in 1493. After the Spanish conquest of the island, the sugar-cane fields were worked by slave labor imported from Africa.

115 top right Hanging over a line attached to a shed, the vegueros' laundry dries in the sun in the countryside of Viñales. The first European to take an interest in tobacco was Columbus, who wrote about receiving it as a gift from an Indian.

116 top A farmer drives his cart to Cárdenas, in Matanzas province, one of the regions with the most sugar-cane plantations. The people of the provinces place a high value on solidarity and cooperation, whereas city life, above all in Havana, seems to increase social isolation.

116 bottom A group of ranchers ride in the Matanzas area. The five million head of Cuban livestock are the property of the state, but at least 80 percent of its three million pigs belong to private farmers.

116-117 An old steam locomotive of American manufacture transports sugar cane.

117 top left A farmer cuts sugar cane.

117 top right Mechanized labor is used in a field in Holguín. With the collapse of the U.S.S.R., motors, pesticides, fertilizers, and fuel became scarce. The sugar-producing industry, second only to Brazil, entered an irreversible crisis.

118-119 The tobacco harvest is underway in Pinar del Río. With a favorable mineral composition in its soil and an average temperature of 77°F, 79 percent humidity, and seasonal rains, Cuba is the most suitable terrain in the world for growing tobacco.

119 top left In Pinar del Río, tobacco is processed and prepared for transport and the first aging stage.

Cigars are composed of three parts: tripa is the internal part, the capote is the sheet that enwraps the tripa, and the capa is the external leaf.

119 top right In the cigar factory of Donatier di Viñales, the work of the torcedor is done by a young woman: with shears, a batten, and vegetable-based glue, she wraps a cigar, producing 200 in 8 hours of work.

118 top left A shed used for processing and aging the crops rises above the tobacco plants in a tobacco field in Pinar del Río. The process of preparing the leaves lasts from 6 to 12 months, but there are also cigars that require leaves aged from 18 months up to three years.

118 top right A farmer lights his cigar in Pinar del Río. The paper labels on cigars were invented to protect the hands of ladies from unattractive nicotine stains, but later on, the strips on cigars came to be appreciated by men as well. With the protective cover, they did not stain their gloves.

118 bottom To transport tobacco, in the Santa Clara area, traditional methods are used. In the cigar factories, there is the reader, who entertains the workers by reading a novel or newspaper. The Romeo and Juliet and Montecristo cigars owe their names to the famous literary works of Dumas and Shakespeare.

The rain forest, where mahogany and ebony trees grow, is not very big but substantial in the high plains and mountains where precipitation levels vary between 100 and 140 inches a year. The most common tree in Cuba is the ceiba (*Ceiba pentandra*), with its enormous trunk and featuring puffy, dense foliage. The most characteristic tree is the royal palm (*Roystonea regia*), a true masterpiece of nature, represented by about 20 million trees reaching up to 130 feet in height. Extremely common are barrigona palms, coconut palms, and various types of ficus. Flame trees (*Royal Poinciana*), imported from Madagascar, and all kinds of tropical plants, including 300 orchid species, prosper. In the numerous national parks, visitors can observe crocodiles, iguanas, lizards, salamanders, sea turtles, and 15 species of non-poisonous snakes such as the boa constrictor, which can reach up to 13 feet long, but which is not dangerous to man. There is even a kind of "living fossil": the *manjuari* (*Atractosteus tristoechus*), also known as the Cuban Alligator Gar because of its semi-reptile appearance. Rodents and bats are common throughout the island as are scorpions and snails. Some 350 bird species can be found, including the Cuban Bee hummingbird, also known as the Helena's hummingbird, the smallest bird in the world; the cattle egret, which spends its time on animals' backs; the turkey vulture; and the *tocororo*, or Cuban trogon, the national bird with its white, red, and blue feathers.

122 top One of the nicest excursions in the Sierra del Escambray is to visit the Salto del Caburni, where one can take a swim in a wild natural setting.

122 bottom Walks leave from Topes de Collantes, in the Sierra del Escambray, and lead to waterways and small lakes surrounded by the luxuriant vegetation of wild fruit trees, royal palms, and orchids, where a wide variety of bird life can be seen.

122-123 Royal palms and crystalline waters characterize the Sierra de Escambray, in the province of Sancti Spiritus. At 2,530 feet tall, there is the health spa of Topes de Collantes, from where climbs to San Juan Peak, at 3,793 feet, and Potrerillo Peak, at 3,055 feet, can be organized.

123 top left A deep river valley opens toward the sea in the province of Pinar del Río.

123 top right In the Zapata Peninsula, in the southern part of Matanzas province, a vast system of swamps and canals extends around the 12 small islands that form Treasure Lagoon, near Guamá, a reconstruction of a Taino Indian village.

124 top left Just beyond the thin strip of cultivated land seen in the lower part of the photo, along the edges of a path, dense forest covers the rises of the Sierra de Escambray, north of Trinidad.

124 top right A waterfall breaks into dozens of little streams in the Sierra de Escambray. On the island, there are 8,000 species of plants,

including cedars, pines, junipers, cork palms, and the Solandra grandiflora.

124-125 The morning mist, in the Viñales Valley, accentuates the poignant beauty of the royal palms. This palm tree, blessed with a thin but strong trunk, symbolizes strength and is an emblem of Cuba.

125 top In the early morning, the night mist lingering low on the ground, a farmer sets off for the fields.

125 bottom Among the infinite variety of trees and cacti, succulent plants, climbing vines, and flowers and orchids present on Cuba, the spine palm can be distinguished by its wide leaves featuring stems covered with sharp thorns.

THE CUBANIA: A UNIQUE CULTURE

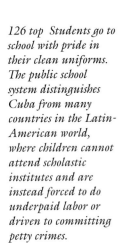

126 top Students go to school with pride in their clean uniforms. The public school system distinguishes Cuba from many countries in the Latin-American world, where children cannot attend scholastic institutes and are instead forced to do underpaid labor or driven to committing petty crimes.

126 bottom A woman looks out her window in a small town in the province of Holguin. In spite of the feminist movement of the 1960s and the struggle for emancipation that pervades society, Cuban women must compete with the male chauvinism of their partners, learned from the old ways of rural culture.

126-127 Men and boys play in a chess club in Remedios, a pretty city in the province of Villa Clara.

Trying to understand the complex Cuban culture means starting from the concept of a "bridge" between several cultural origins: Native American, Spanish, Galician, Catalan, African (Yoruba from Nigeria, that of Benin) as well as Haitian, Caribbean, and Chinese – just to name a few of its many roots. It is no accident that the most extraordinary Cuban magazine of the 1950s, edited by the intellectual José Lezama Lima, was called *Origenes* and analyzed the Cuban identity's position within the universal debate. Cuba must be seen in consideration of the entire Latin American cultural area, the influence of Europe, and exposure to ideas that have come from North America throughout the twentieth century. After the 1959 revolution, the United States became the great global enemy, though for many Cubans the United States was a way out, a forbidden dream, a point of reference, or an alternative. History and Cuban sentiment, ancient divisions between masters and slaves, complicated racial relations, rediscovered solidarity in the fight against foreign domination, the battles for equality generated by the revolution, and the internationalist experiences that the Cubans had in Africa must all be examined. Imperialism, colonialism, cravings for independence, love of one's country, the desire for economic and cultural freedom, and Marxism: Cuba has consumed all the ideologies of the world. The experience of suffering under colonial domination has pushed Cubans to seek the theories offered by the great ideological movements. Today, however, the contemporary world forces them to accept a daily compromise between living and looking to a future that reflects the dialectical country saying, "tomorrow is another day." In fact – it being understood that Havana is a case apart – the foundations of Cuban society are essentially rural. Thus, the Cuban cultural and religious mix is a syncretism that embraces everything with the typical diffidence of country folk for whom the horizon finishes at the end of the tilled field and the rhythms of life are those determined by the cutting of the sugar cane. Yet, that is the tragedy: to be the offspring of the culture of one's overlord and discover, in the moment of liberation, that one falls right back into patterns prefabricated by the outside world; first, colonial religions and ideologies, and then Marxism, born of Hegelian, German, and European historicism.

127 top center Many turn to healers (in the photo, a healer from the province of Villa Clara) and santeros in an attempt to improve their life.

127 top right A worshipper prays in a church in Camagüey. In Cuba, a citizen can ascribe to a religion, but cannot put it before the Constitution or the defense of the country.

To understand the Cuba of today, try imagining any European country having been subjected to the same fate of servitude and destruction, deportation and exploitation. Try deciding whether or not out of such a convoluted series of tragic events that had erased any and all identities, mixing up traits as if in a blender, the identity of a people would then be born. Out of this dramatic past, the Cuban people brought forth a proud vengeance born in the form of their own diversity. From this intense labor, Cuba extracted inspiring writings, such as the great works of litera-

Catholic Church baptized them by force. However, they were allowed to dance and play music. The slaves matched their own *orisha* divinities to the Catholic saints, according to their characteristics. Changó, the *orisha* of thunder, fire, and light was associated with Santa Barbara. Yemayá, the *orisha* of the sea, was paired with the Our Lady of Regla. Oshun, the *orisha* of love, entertainment, and sweetness, was identified with Our Lady of Charity of Cobre, becoming the patron saint of Cuba, with her copper-colored face. Babalé Aye, who comforts the sick, became Saint Lazarus.

ture by Alejo Carpentier, an author that effectively embodies Cuban culture in as much as his "marvelous reality" of the Latin-American identity is the fruit of multiple overlapping aspects that together form an intricate, unpredictable, elaborate, and incredible cultural picture. For Cubans, it means discovering their own hidden identity and even pride in a "differentness" that they have known how to acquire from the various cultures without, however, letting themselves be conquered. The Cuban literary world is cultured and varied, boasting the poetry of Nicolás Guillén, Gaston Baguero, and Eliseo Diego; the short stories of Onelio Jorge Cardoso; the intimism of Dulce Maria Loynaz; the dark pessimism of Ana Lidia Vega; and the feminine identity found in the work of Alba de Céspedes, the half-Italian author well known in Europe. The unique character of Cuban culture can be found by studying the origin of the island's music. Centuries ago, slaves could not practice their native religions; the

Religious rituals were based on music and dance, beginning with dances like the *guancà*, the *yambé*, the columbia, and various types of rumba, to which, from the 1920s on, modern instrumental accompaniments were added. In Cuba, thanks to the musical syncretism resulting from the blend of African customs with Spanish and European ones, the large-orchestra rumba, *son*, *danzón*, mambo, cha-cha-chá, bolero, and habañera were born. Today, along with the more recently developed *merengue*, salsa, and *timba*, these dances constitute a large portion of what humans around the planet have danced. In fact, while the tunes of Company Segundo and the film *Buena Vista Social Club* are only played in the tourist traps of Havana, the *timba*, closely tied to Afro-American music from the United States, is popular in the "lower" working-class neighborhoods of the city and is characterized by the sensational effect of live performances and its unconventionality. Groups like Luis Cortes' "NG la

129 top left In the field of music, Cuba possesses a complex array of exceptional forms of expression, and its musicians, a sensitivity for sound that has been fine-tuned over the centuries and an innate sense of rhythm.

129 top right A group of trapeze artists in Havana stroll through the streets of the old city on stilts, accompanied by their own collection of instruments.

banda" and David Calzado's "Gharanga Habañera" have made a radical break from the nostalgic music played by the nice old men of Company Segundo and, with a rhythmic explosive energy, speak of racism, sex, tourism, and money. Deep changes are happening in the world of theater, film, and the visual arts. The last Latin-American Festival of the Cinema, in December 2003 in Havana, was won by the film *Suite Habana* by director Fernando Pérez, author of works such as *Clandestinos, Hello Hemingway*, and *La vida es silbar*, which received the Flaiano Prize in Italy in 2000. The names of other directors such as Juan Carlos Tabio, Tomas Gutierrez Aléa (the creator of *Strawberries and Chocolate*), and Humberto Solas are known throughout the world. In art, the rising star of painter Alexis "Kcho," the product of a school including names such as Wilfredo Lam, René Portocarrero, Amelia Peláez, and Manuel Mendive, shines brightly, whereas many talented young people are making their mark in a veritable boom in figurative art that is sweeping the island. Cuba is also famous for high levels of achievement in all types of sports. At every meeting of the Olympic Games, this small nation of few means repeatedly surprises the world by earning medals: at the 2000 Games in Sidney, Cuba won 29 medals, of which 11 were gold. Finally, Cuba is the world capital of cocktails, which are enjoyed all around the world. Here, some of the most famous cocktails were invented. They can be drunk leaning against a late-19th-century bar while a couple dances an old rumba and the sun paints a sensual sunset over the sea: this is the marvelous island.

INDEX

Note: *c = caption*

A

Acosta, Rafael, 47c
Africa, 11, 28c, 29c, 114c, 126
Agabama River, 121c
Agramonte, Ignacio, 30, 79c
Agramonte, Ignacio, Park, *see* Camagüey
Alegría de Pío, 36
Alexis "Kcho," 130
Alvarado, Pedro de, 22
America, 22c, 25c, 85c, 86c, 88c
Ancón Peninsula, 106
Angola, 29c, 44
Antonelli, Giovanni Battista, 47, 73
Argentina, 37c
Asia, 8
Atlantic Ocean, 25c

B

Bacardi, Facundo, 57c
Baconao Park, 104
Baconao River, 104
Baghero, Gaston, 128
Bahamas, 108c
Bahia de Cochinos (Bay of Pigs), 14c, 42c, 43, 43c
Bahia de Nipe, 15c
Balboa, Silvestre de, 25
Baracoa, 15c, 75, 75c, 77c, 88
  Cathedral of Our Lady of Assumption, 75c
Baraguá, 30
Bariay, 8
Batista, Fulgencio, 11c, 34, 35c, 36, 37, 38, 52c, 69c
Bayamo, 25, 30, 75, 88
Benin, 130c
Bernhart, Sarah, 49c
Birán, 75
Bobadilla, Isabel de, 47
Bolivia, 43
Borromini, Francesco, 61
Boston, 27
Brazil, 116c
Bush, George W., 44

C

Caburní, salto del, 122c
Caibarién, 15c
Calzado, David, 130
Camagüey Archipelago, 15c
Camagüey, 7c, 15c, 30, 79, 79c, 80c, 85c, 100, 106, 127, 129c
  Academy of San Alejandro, 80c
  Basilica of Our Lady of Mercy, 79c
  Cemetery Square, 79c

Church of the Holy Christ of Travels, 79c
  Ignazio Agramonte Park, 79c
  Plaza de Armas, 79, 79c
  Plaza del Carmen, 79
  Plaza San Juan de Dios, 79
Camarón Grande, 100
Canada, 27
Canary Islands, 25, 30c
Cardenas, 14c, 116c
Cardoso, Onelio Jorge, 128
Caribbean Sea, 100, 100c
Caribbean, the, 25c, 34, 47, 82c, 98c
Carpentier, Alejo, 14, 61, 67, 75c, 128
Caruso, Enrico, 94
Castile, 22c
Castro, Angel, 36
Castro, Fidel, 12, 36, 36c, 37, 37c, 38, 38c, 43, 43c, 44c, 45c, 50, 61c, 67, 70, 75c, 85
Castro, Raúl, 37, 38c
Caunao, 15c
Cauto, 15c
Cayo Blanco, 104c
Cayo Coco, 7c, 8c, 15c, 100, 104, 106, 108c, 110c, 111c, 113c
Cayo Guillermo, 104, 104c
Cayo Largo del Sur, 106
Cayo Levisa, 106
Cayo Romano, 15c, 100
Cayo Santa Maria, 106
Céspedes, Alba de, 128
Céspedes, Carlos Manuel de, 30, 75
Chacón, Don Luis, 61, 65c
Charles III, 27
Charles V, 25c
Chartrand, Esteban, 91
Churchill, Winston, 69c
Ciao Milena: mi sono dimenticata di correggere la voce di Khrushchev nell'indice (e rimasta evidenziata appunto perche
Ciego de Ávila, 8c, 15c, 79, 82c, 104c, 106, 106c
  Bank of Credit and Commerce, 82c
Cienfuegos, 14c, 15c, 94, 96c, 97c
  Government Hall, 97c
  José Martí Park, 96c, 97c
  Palacio del Valle, 96c
  Punta Gorda, 97c
Cinco Palmas, 36c
Cisneros, Salvador, 31c
Clinton, Bill, 44
Columbus, Christopher, 8, 14, 22c, 25, 75c, 85c, 114c
Compostela, Diego de, 50, 61c
Cortés, Hernan, 22, 22c, 70

Cortés, Luis, 130
Cuchillas de Toa, 75c

D

Dahomey, 130c
Delarra, José, 85c
Diego, Eliseo, 128
Dominican Republic, the, 38
Drake, Francis, 25, 27c, 63c
Duaba River, 77c
Dumas, Alexandre, 118c

E

El Yunque, 15c
England, 25, 27
Espín, Vilma, 37
Estrada Palma, Tómas, 34c
Ethiopia, 44
Europe, 11, 29, 128

F

Ferdinand d'Aragona, 8
Finca Duaba, 77c
Finca Las Mañacas, 75
Finca Vigia, 69, 69c
Florida, 27, 43, 44, 47, 136c
Flynn, Errol, 75c
France, 25, 27
Fuentes, Norberto, 63c

G

Gaggini, Giuseppe, 61
Garcia Lorca, Federico, 49c
Garcia, Calisto, 11c, 31c
Gardner, Ava, 69c
Girón, Gilberto, 25
Gomez Baez, Maximo, 11, 30, 31c, 32, 54c, 73c
Gomez, Panchito, 32
Goyri, Amelia, 67
Grau San Martín, Ramón, 34
Great Britain, 27
Green, Graham, 49
Grijalba, Juan de, 22
Grillo, Diego, 25
Guamá, 122c
Guamuhaya Sierra, 114
Guaniguanico Cordillera, 114c
Guantánamo, 15c, 32, 104, 130c
Guardalavaca, 104
Guatemala, 25c, 37, 43
Guevara, Ernesto, alias "Che," 11c, 14, 37, 37c, 38, 38c, 43, 47c, 50, 58c, 61c, 67, 67c, 75c, 85, 85c
Guillén, Nicolás, 128
Guisa, 38
Gutierrez Aléa, Tomas, 130

H

Haiti, 27, 88, 130c
Hatuey, 25

Havana, 7c, 11c, 12, 14c, 15c, 25c, 26c, 27, 27c, 29, 29c, 30, 32, 34, 35c, 36, 38c, 42c, 43, 44c, 45c, 47, 47c, 49, 50, 51c, 52c, 54c, 57, 57c, 58c, 61, 61c, 63c, 65c, 67, 69c, 70, 80c, 85c, 100c, 116c, 126, 128, 128c, 129c, 130
  Academy of Sciences, 50, 50c
  Bacardi Palace, 56c
  Banco Nacional, 52c
  Bodeguita del Medio, 61, 63c
  Capitol, the, 15c, 49c, 50, 50c, 51c, 52, 61
  Castillo de la Real Fuerza, 47
  Colón Monumentale Cemetery, 67, 67c
  Commerce Department, 57c, 61, 61c
  El Morro, 27, 46, 47c
  El Morro, lighthouse, 47c
  El Patio, 61, 65c
  Floridita, 61, 63c
  Grand Theater, 50, 52c
  Granma Pavilion, 50
  Hotel Ambos Mundos, 61
  Hotel Inglaterra, 49, 49c
  Hotel Nacional, 47c, 69, 69c
  Hotel Plaza, 52c
  Hotel Sevilla, 49
  La Fuerza, 27
  La Punta, 27
  Malecón, 11c, 47c, 54, 54c, 57, 69, 69c
  Marquises of Aguas Claras, residence of, 61, 65c
  Miramar, 69
  Museum of Colonial Art, 65c
  Museum of Fine Arts, 50
  Museum of the City of Havana, 65c
  Museum of the Revolution, 50, 52c
  National Library of Cuba, 50c, 51c
  Old Square, 56c
  Palacio de los Capitanes Generales, 61, 65c
  Palacio de los Matrimonios, 49c
  Palacio del Segundo Cabo, 61
  Park of the Martyrs of '71, 55c
  Parque Central, 49, 49c, 52c
  Paseo de Martí, 49, 49c, 51c, 52
  Plaza des Armas, 47, 57c, 61, 61c, 65c
  Real Fabrica de Tabacos La Corona, 49c
  San Carlo de la Cabaña, fortress of, 47
  San Cristóbal, cathedral of, 61

134

San Francesco d'Assisi Square, 61, 61c
San Francesco d'Assisi, church of, 61
Santo Ángel Custodio, church of, 50
Seminary of Saints Carlos e Ambrose, 47c
Teatro Amedeo Roldan, 52c
Tropicana, 69c
Vedado, 67, 67c, 69, 69c
Hemingway, Ernest, 14, 61, 63c, 69, 69c, 104c, 106
Hemingway, Marina, 69
Heredia, José Maria, 29
Hernandez, Melba, 36
Hicacos Peninsula, 136c
Holguín, 11c, 15c, 30, 75, 75c, 100, 104, 116c, 126c
Holland, 25
Hotel La Rusa, 75c

I
India, 27
Ingenios Valley, 12c, 88, 88c
Isabella de Castile, 8
Isla de la Juventud, 14c, 100, 106
Isla de Pinos, 121c
Italy, 69c, 130
Iznaga, Pedro, 88

J
Jamaica, 27, 82c, 88
Jatibonica, 121c
Jibacoa, 100c
John Paul II, pope, 44, 44c

K
Kennedy, John Fitzgerald, 42c, 43
Khrushchev, Nikita Sergeyevich, 43c

L
Lam, Wilfredo, 130
Las Cabezas Altamirano, Juan de, 25
Las Casas, Bartolomé de, 25, 25c
Las Coloradas, 36c
Las Tunas, 15c
Lazare, Luis, 25c
Lescay, Alberto, 71c
Lezama Lima, José, 126
Lima, 27
Lopez, Narciso, 30
Los Canarreos Archipelago, 100, 106
Los Jardines de la Reina, 15c, 100, 106
Loynaz, Dulce Maria, 128

M
Maceo, Antonio, 30, 31c, 32, 49c, 71c, 73, 73c
Machado, Gerardo, 34, 34c, 35c, 50, 69c
MacKinley, William, 32c
Madrid, Ferdinando, 29
Magellano, 25c

Mantes, Pedro, 28c
Marea del Portillo, 104
Mariel Bay, 100
Mariel Port, 27
Martí, José, 30, 30c, 31c, 32, 49, 50, 67, 67c, 73c, 82c, 86c
Martí, José, Park, see Cienfuegos
Martí, Paseo de, see Havana
Martinez, Angel, 63c
Martinique, 73
Matanzas, 14c, 27, 94, 98c, 100c, 116c, 122c
Matthews, Herbert L., 38
Mayarí, 36
Mediterranean Sea, 100c
Melodioso River, 12c, 121c
Mendive, Manuel, 130
Menghistu, 44
Mexico City, 27
Mexico, 22c, 25c, 37, 37c, 70
Mexico, Gulf of, 100
Miami, 43, 43c, 44
Moa, 15c
Mogote dos Hermanas, 12c
Montezuma, 22c
Morgan Henry, 25, 70
Morón, 15c, 82c
Moscow, 43

N
Najasa, 15c
Narváez, Pánfilo de, 22
Nassau, 108c
Nau, François, alias l'Olonnais, 25
Nemours, Dupont de, 106c
Neto, Agostinho, 44
New York, 27, 28c, 31c, 43c
Nicaragua, 43
Nuestra Assunción de Baracoa, 25
Nueva Gerona, 14c

O
Ocampo, Sebastián de, 22
Oviedo, Fernandez de, 114

P
Pacific Ocean, 25c
Paris, 32c
Peláez, Amelia, 130
Pérez, Fernando, 130
Perovani, Giuseppe, 61
Perù, 25c
Philippines, 32c
Picco de Potrerillo, 122c
Picco San Juan, 114, 122c
Piñar del Rio, 12c, 14c, 34, 106, 114, 114c, 118c, 122c
Placetas, 14c, 86c
Playa Ancón, 104c
  Girón, 43, 100c
  Juragua, 100c
  Larga, 43
  Paredon, 106c
  Sirena, 106
Plaza of the Rooster, 82c
Ponce, Fidelio, 79c
Portillo, César, 14
Portocarrero, René, 14, 130

Portsmouth, 27
Portugal, 25
Prieto, Abel, 67
Prío Socarrás, Carlos, 34
Puerto Rico, 32c
Punta Maisì, 104

R
Remedios, 94, 126c
Rio Chaviano, 36c
Rodriguez, Lester, 37
Rome, 61
Rosario de Santa Fé, 37c
Rousseau, Jean-Jacques, 25
Rovieskuya, Magdalena, 75c
Ruiz, José, 28c
Russia, 12
Ruz González, Lina, 36

S
Sabana Archipelago, 14c
Salas, Esteban, 70c
San Cristobal de la Habana, 25, 47
San Juan, 14c
San Pedro, 32
San Salvador, 8
Sanchez Echevarria, Francisco, 73c
Sanchez, Celia, 37
Sanchez, Serafin, 94c
Sancti Spiritus, 12c, 15c, 25, 94, 94c, 114c, 121c, 122c
  Puente Yayabo, 94, 94c
Santa Barbara, 14c
Santa Clara, 11c, 14c, 85, 85c, 118c
  Basilica of Our Lady of Travels, 85c
  Plaza Mayor, 11c
  Plaza Vidal, 85c
  Revolution Square, 85, 85c
Santa Fé, 14c
Santa Maria de Puerto Principe, 25
Santamaría, Abel, 36
Santamaría, Haidée, 36, 37
Santiago de Cuba, 15c, 25, 27, 30, 36, 37, 38c, 57c, 70, 70c, 73, 73c, 97c, 100c, 104, 128c
  Castillo del Morro, 73
  Cemetery of Santa Santiago de Ifigenia, 73c
  Céspedes Park, 70
  El Morro Fortress, 27
  Emilio Bacardi Museum, 73
  House of Traditions, 73
  Plaza de Marte, 73c
Santisima Trinidad, 25
Santo Domingo, 22, 30
Sartia, Pedro, 36c
Segundo, Company, 128, 130
Senegal, 29c
Shakespeare, William, 118c
Sidney, 130
Sierra de los Organos, 14c
  de Escambray, 14c, 15c, 122c, 125c

del Rosario, 14c, 114c
  Leone (Africa), 28c
  Maestra, 15c, 38, 104
Sinatra, Frank, 69c
Slave Coast, 130c
Solás, Humberto, 130
Somalia, 44
Somoza, Luis, 43
Sores, Jacques de, 47, 70
Soto, Hernando de, 47
South Africa, 44
Soviet Union, 43, 43c, 44, 67c, 100c, 116c, 136c
Spain, 8, 25, 25c, 27, 29, 30, 32, 54c, 69c, 79, 126
Stevenson, Robert Louis, 121c
Sumner Welles, Benjamin, 35c

T
Tabio, Juan Carlos, 130
Toa, 15c, 75c
Topes de Collantes, 106, 122c
Trinidad, 14c, 30c, 88, 88c, 91c, 92c, 104c, 121c, 125c, 126c, 130c
  Brunet Manor, 91, 92c
  History Museum, 92c
  Holy Trinity, church of the, 91, 91c
  Plaza Mayor, 91, 91c

U
United States of America, 12, 27, 29, 30, 32, 32c, 34, 35c, 38, 38c, 42c, 43, 44, 51c, 54c, 57c, 69c, 126
Urrutia, Manuel, 38

V
Valdés, Cecilia, 50
Valencia (Spain), 30c
Varadero, 8c, 14c, 98c, 106, 106c, 113c, 136c
Varela, Felix, 29
Vega, Ana Lidia, 128
Velásquez de Cuellar, Diego, 22, 22c, 25, 70, 70c, 75
Venice, 65c
Villa Clara, 86c, 126c, 127c
Villaverde, Cirilo, 50
Viñales Valley, 12c, 114c, 125c
Viñales, 14c, 114
Von Humboldt, Alexander Friedrich, 91

W
Washington, 32, 43, 51c
Weiler, 31c
Wright, Irene, 27c

Y
Yayabo, Puente, see Sancti Spiritus

Z
Zanelli, Angelo, 50c
Zapata Peninsula, 14c, 122c
Zaza, 121c

136 Facing onto the Strait of Florida, the Peninsula de Hicacos has the most popular and famous tourist resort in Cuba: Varadero. For years frequented by an elite tourism from the Communist Bloc, after the collapse of the Soviet Union, it started to attract an international array of visitors. Thanks to places like Varadero, Cuba's "new path" was launched.